ARE THERE TWO POWERS IN HEAVEN?

BY
CHRISTOPHER MONAGHAN

Cry Out Ministries International
P.O. Box 103
Webster, IN 47392

Printed in the United States of America

DEDICATION

I dedicate this book to the fearless reformers throughout history who have held firmly to the word of God and to truth despite the cost

TABLE OF CONTENTS

Chapter 1   Jesus Has Landed

Chapter 2   Bad Chronology

Chapter 3   New Wineskins

Chapter 4   Be a Berean

Chapter 5   Need an Adapter?

Chapter 6   Royal Succession

Chapter 7   Another Power?

Chapter 8   Dabar Yahweh

Chapter 9   Covenant Maker

Chapter 10 Behold a Son!

Chapter 11 Son of Man

Chapter 12 Son of God

Chapter 13 The Narrative

Chapter 14 Love Sacrifice

Chapter 15 Son Succession

Chapter 16 Monotheism

Chapter 17 The Title of God

Chapter 18 Strict Monotheism

Chapter 19 Echad

Chapter 20 No Other Gods

Chapter 21 Yahweh ≠ Trinity

Chapter 22 Angel-Yahweh

Chapter 23 Compound Words

Chapter 24 My Father's Name

Chapter 25 Who is Who?

Chapter 26 See Him and Die

Chapter 27 Prophecy Fulfilled

Chapter 28 Christophany

Chapter 29 Who is "I AM"

Chapter 30 Jesus is Lord

Chapter 31 The Messiah

Chapter 32 Servant of Yahweh

Chapter 33 Unveiled

Chapter 34 Yahweh Saves

Chapter 35 Modalism

Chapter 36 Lamb Forever

Chapter 37 Choose a Lamb Day

Chapter 38 Handle the Blood

Chapter 39 Marry the Lamb

Chapter 40 The New King

Chapter 41 Moving Air

Chapter 42 Flesh and Spirit

Chapter 43 Not a Ghost

Chapter 44 No Name

Chapter 45 Separate Person?

Chapter 46 Of Father and Son

Chapter 47 Baptize in the Name

Chapter 48 First Mention

Chapter 49 Gender Bender

Chapter 50 Spirit Pronouns

Chapter 51 Power to Change

Chapter 52 Pronoun Swap

Chapter 53 No Third Person

Chapter 54 Rules of Grammar

Chapter 55 John or Paul?

Chapter 56 Three's a Crowd

Chapter 57 Forgotten God

Chapter 58 Real Orthodoxy

Chapter 59 Cause of Heresy

Chapter 60 God Substance

Chapter 61 Relation Emphasis

Chapter 62 One Mediator Only

Chapter 63 Tinted Glasses

Chapter 64 Jesus Be the Center

Chapter 65 Jewish Barriers

Chapter 66 Electric Fences

Chapter 67 Nourishing Sap

Chapter 68 Stumbling Stone

Chapter 69 Intolerance

Chapter 70 One New Man

Chapter 71 Antisemitism

Chapter 72 Dispensationalism

Chapter 73 Prophet Like Moses

Chapter 74 Book of Enoch

Chapter 75 Indestructible Jew

Chapter 76 Father Abraham

Chapter 77 Promise to Nations

Chapter 78 Mosaic Covenant

Chapter 79 Israel's Call

Chapter 80 Joseph's Ascension

Chapter 81 Joseph Unveiled

Chapter 82 Self-Persecution

Chapter 83 Grafted In

Chapter 84 Israel's Destiny

Chapter 85 Cycle Kingdom

Chapter 86 One Throne

Chapter 87 Christology

Chapter 88 Renewed Covenant

Chapter 89 The Ascension

Chapter 90 The B Team

Chapter 91 God Encounters

Chapter 92 Awakening

Chapter 93 Your Name Please?

Chapter 94 A Dim Mirror

Chapter 95 Conclusion

Chapter One

JESUS HAS LANDED

Jesus, when he came, came in a form that many, many Jews were expecting: a second divine figure incarnated in a human. The question was not "Is a divine Messiah coming?" but only "Is this carpenter from Nazareth the One we are expecting?"[1]
Daniel Boyarin

As a new believer at Penn State University, I began taking classes on religion, and one of the first books I read was by a Jewish scholar named Alan Segal. Though Jewish, he wrote a lot about Christianity and its Jewish influences. His most notable work was a book titled "Two Powers in Heaven." Segal's writings planted a seed in me that has grown into a fruitful tree over these last thirty years and motivated me to write this book.

From my understanding, I assumed that the Jewish theologians throughout history were deeply committed to the strictest of monotheism. Alan Segal's research revealed that Jewish religious thought during the time of Jesus embraced another power in heaven.

Re-reading the New Testament with a two-power paradigm in mind has been a refreshing experience. As if scales have fallen off my eyes, I see that Jews had entertained and even embraced the idea of another power in heaven. Only after the death, burial, and resurrection of Jesus did the rabbis exchange the two powers in heaven paradigm for a strict form of

[1] Boyarin, Daniel. The Jewish Gospels . The New Press. Kindle Edition

monotheism to dissuade other Jews from following Jesus. Because Jesus powerfully fulfilled the Messianic expectations of Judaism, many Jewish religious leaders deemed any acceptance of a second power in heaven as heresy.

The early disciples had no problem worshipping Jesus as King. They accepted his position in heaven the same way they saw Yahweh's position. Jesus had a God license just like Yahweh. Yet, at this point, what I define as strict monotheism(i.e., the belief in only one God) falls apart. Two powers in heaven **cannot be** monotheism because **Jesus + Father = 2.**

FROM A BIBLICAL PERSPECTIVE ALONE, YAHWEH USUALLY ASSUMED THE TITLE AS GOD AND JESUS USUALLY ASSUMED THE TITLE OF LORD. JESUS IS THE ETERNAL SON OF GOD WHO SITS ON THE THRONE OF HIS FATHER. JEWS WHO OPPOSED JESUS CLAIMS FIERCELY RESPONDED AGAINST HIS FOLLOWERS BECAUSE OF THOROUGHNESS IN WHICH HE FULFILLED THE EXPECTATIONS OF THE MESSIAH. THE DENIAL OF BELIEVING IN TWO POWERS IN HEAVEN WAS THE FIRST STEP TO DELEGITIMIZE HIS CLAIMS .

Chapter Two

BAD CHRONOLOGY

Many years ago, my family and I visited Antietam, Maryland's great civil war battlefield. The park ranger giving us the tour told us a funny story about a question someone asked one time after the tour. They asked, *"How is it that almost all the major civil war battles occurred on National Park Lands?"* (They did not realize that the battlefield was later dedicated to being set apart as National Park Land). The park ranger jokingly commented, *"Because of the free camping, I imagine!"* The chronology of this person assumed the parks existed before the Civil War; hence this person had come to strange conclusions. When we better understand the chronology(i.e., the timing) of events, we can better grasp the writings of the New Testament.

Rabbi Daniel Boyarin writes about the Jews of this period who *"...believed that God had a divine deputy or emissary or even son, exalted above all the angels, who functioned as an intermediary between God and the world."*[2] This belief seemed to fit Christianity like the glass slipper fit on Cinderella's foot. The rabbis who did not accept the claims of Jesus responded by erasing any views of a second power in heaven. As Christian theology developed over the centuries, many early church fathers never embraced

---

[2] Boyarin, Daniel. The Jewish Gospels . The New Press. Kindle Edition

the idea of a second power in heaven because they did not know it existed. The thesis of this book is that Jews in the times of Jesus had a well-developed "two powers" narrative based on the 7th chapter of Daniel, yet later denied its validity as Christianity blossomed.

Up to the destruction of the Temple in 70 A.D, Christianity was a sect of Judaism. The Temple was the center of Judaism until it was torn down, and from that time forward, strong borderlines were drawn between Christianity and Judaism. The denial of Jesus as the Messiah and the chosen second power of heaven became the dividing issue. One way to minimize Jesus was to reduce the role he claimed to have. Jewish thought developed into a strict, unbending monotheism that left no room for Jesus on the throne.

In the centuries that followed, as Jews and Christians debated, the Jew would insult the Christian and label them a polytheist. Christian apologists reacted to this label in error instead of responding to the idea of a second power in heaven. Christian theologians later developed the concept of the Trinity, which embraces monotheism and allows Jesus to be distinct from Yahweh(and the Spirit). Yet the danger of the Trinity is losing the distinction between the Father and the Son.

MANY THEOLOGIANS FAIL TO MAKE A CLEAR DISTINCTION BETWEEN GOD THE FATHER AND THE SON OF GOD,

---

Chapter Three

NEW WINESKINS

Jesus reminded us of the importance of preparing a "new wineskin" in preparation for the new wine.

And no one pours new wine into old wineskins. If he does, the wine will burst the skins, and both the wine and the wineskins will be ruined. No, he pours new wine into new wineskins (Mark 2:22 NIV).

Today we place wine in glass bottles, but in ancient times, wine was placed in pouches made of animal stomachs. When a new stomach was used, it could be stretched as the wine inside of it fermented. New wine is a wine that is not fermented. Thus, a wine that is old and fermented can be stored in old wineskins without any concern. But if someone poured new wine into an old wineskin, it would ruin the wineskin because it can no longer stretch and make room for fermentation.

Pouring new wine into an old wineskin will ruin both the new wine and the old wineskin. The ancients had a process of running new wine over the old wineskins, which readied the skin for new wine.

You might deem this writing as unbiblical when you are being stretched. Sometimes we do not discern between false teaching and wineskin stretching, but I challenge you to test your thinking. In fear of bursting the old wineskin, you might feel like rejecting the new wine. It will help to let go of your old mindset because it will not hold the living, fermenting wine poured out this season.

This book is not new information but instead a paradigm shift. And this paradigm is not a new revelation of mine but rather a newly discovered revelation that many Jews embraced in the time of Christ. Remember, a paradigm is a thought process, a pattern of thinking, or a worldview that will redefine every fact or piece of information that enters its system. It is the backdrop or playing board which, you see the world and the pattern you base your core values upon, or the glasses from which you view life. Your "paradigm" is what must be impacted when you come to Christ.

Our paradigms can be like old wineskins that will burst unless we soak them first with new wine. That is why Jesus told us to repent– "change our paradigm," the Greek word *metanoe*. *Meta* means "change" and *noe* means "mind."

You have accomplished an excellent task when you help someone change their paradigm. When our paradigm is challenged, it may feel like we are trying to turn our steering wheel without power steering fluid or guide an obstinate animal we are riding. We must not just receive the facts we are hearing but also embrace the new paradigm.

The best way I can explain a paradigm is as follows: Imagine trying to play football on a baseball field. You are trying to follow the rules of football, but nothing seems to fit together.

Yet, move the teams to a football field, and everything seems to work. This is what a paradigm shift will accomplish.

I pray that the church remembers her roots and identifies with her Hebraic mindset. I recognize that change does not come easily. You may initially experience discomfort, but I hope you will open your mind to new ways of thinking and that this book will provide a new wineskin for you to hold the new wine.

In 2010, I released my first book, "Heaven's Dynasty." The book focused on how the ancients were very familiar with the concept of a king establishing a dynasty for the next generation. Every kingdom would continue generation after generation because a son would succeed his Father as King. Every mighty King longed for a son sitting on his throne and carrying on his legacy after he died.

"Are There Two Powers in Heaven?" is a book that suggests the emphasis of the Old and New Testaments is to present two powers in heaven: a Father and a Son. I propose that this was a prominent view among the Jews in the times of Jesus. I also suggest that the writers of the New Testament fully embraced the idea of a second power in heaven, where Judaism would later emphasize one power and Christians would emphasize three powers.

A GOOD SON RULES IN THE IMAGE AND CHARACTER OF HIS FATHER, ENSURING THAT THE THRONE WILL ENDURE.

Chapter Four

BE A BEREAN

Over the last fifty years, two prominent Jewish scholars, Alan Segal and Daniel Boyarin, have made strong arguments that the idea of two powers existing in heaven was the primary belief among many Jews in the time of Jesus. Later Jewish thought, after the destruction of the Temple, then shifted to declare the view of two powers in heaven as heretical and began emphasizing the oneness of God. This book will lead you on a journey to see Jesus as the other power in heaven, the role He claimed while on earth. His power was that of a Son who would rule on the throne of His Father.

The pivotal moment in Jewish history was the destruction of the Temple in the year 70 C.E.(A.D.) Judaism had to transform itself into a meaningful religion without its Temple. Rabbis got together and developed a form of Judaism called Rabbinical Judaism, and this Judaism is much different than what was called Temple Judaism. Christianity is older than Rabbinical Judaism. Paul and Silas escaped from Thessalonica after an uprising due to their other teaching. When they arrived at Berea, Luke writes:

"The brothers immediately sent Paul(*Small*) and Silas(*Of the forest*) away by night to Berea(*Stable*). When they arrived, they went into the Jewish synagogue. Now these Jews were more

noble than those in Thessalonica*(Victory over falsehood);* **they received the word with all eagerness, examining the Scriptures daily to see if these things were so."**

(Acts 17:11 TNT)

Oddly enough, Thessalonica means "victory over falsehood," yet the Jews there violently chased the messengers of truth away. The Jews of Berea were declared noble because they examined the Scriptures daily. Berea means "stable," and without our daily bread, we will not have stability in our lives. Someone once said, "Grow daily or die gradually."

I have spent decades meditating and studying the Scriptures, attempting to discern the paradigm of the first Jewish disciples of Jesus. I viewed the relationship between the Father, the Son, and Spirit in a manner that often resulted in confusion. I believed one way, but when I read the Bible, my view of the Father, Son, and Spirit felt forced and not natural. I have concluded that the lack of Hebraic thought on the formation of doctrinal issues in Christianity proved detrimental.

"Are There Two Powers in Heaven?" seeks to understand best the mindset of the writers of the New Testament. They understood Jesus was not Yahweh, but He was the Messiah, the One sent by Him to be fully King! Every King longed to have a faithful Son to rule on his throne.

Chapter Five

NEED AN ADAPTER?

In the United States, most electrical devices have a two-pronged plug inserted into a two-pronged outlet. Yet some electrical devices have a three-pronged plug that requires a two-pronged adapter to fit into a typical outlet. When dealing with this issue, I had to find the source of the problem:

1. **The two-pronged outlets should be three-pronged**
2. **Electrical devices should always be two-pronged**
3. **Two-pronged adapters must be readily available**

Was the problem the electrical outlets, the electronic devices, or the lack of the two-pronged adapter? The power source is the electric outlet and is a picture of the God-given narrative in the Scriptures that presents a two-power throne. Many high-powered electronic devices fashioned with a three-pronged plug represent believers who accepted the doctrine of a God in three persons. The adapter allows three-pronged devices to receive power from a two-pronged outlet. The intense teaching and indoctrination of the Trinity over the past 1700 years is a picture of this adapter. The adapter allows the Scriptures to be understood through the Trinity, though this doctrine is unnecessarily complex and rarely understood.

As I studied at a Messianic Jewish Bible school in my thirties, I discovered the lenses I needed to see the Scriptures from a Jewish perspective– a perspective almost completely lost within the first two centuries of the church. Without its Hebrew roots, Christianity soon began to find its footing in Greek philosophy. The most influential theologians of Christianity, St. Augustine and Thomas Aquinas, were both highly skilled philosophers who have shaped our theology to this today.

The doctrine of the Trinity was the most outstanding achievement of this philosophical influence. This doctrine has persevered throughout Christian history, establishing Jesus as God like His Father without violating monotheism's sacred principle. But to be clear, I am not applauding the influence of Greek philosophy. Jesus was accepted as "Lord" by the early Christians, but His place of honor was no different than that of Yahweh. The creeds later established by the church strayed far from the simple confession that "Jesus is Lord!"

The argument of this book is to show from Scripture, and recent Jewish rabbinical scholarship, that the apostle John, Paul, and the other disciples of Jesus adhered to the paradigm that there were two powers in heaven. I believe this is the most Biblical paradigm and is theologically more substantial than other core beliefs in Christianity.

Many theologians inform us that the relationship between God the Father, Jesus Christ, and the function of the Holy Spirit is 'mysterious.' In my experience, requiring Christians to embrace the Trinity has instilled confusion instead of simplicity. But emphasizing Unitarianism may lessen the person of Jesus Christ to its followers. There is a ditch on either side of the road.

This book is my attempt at providing a framework for our thinking about the kingdom that will ground our message in the core understanding of God as Father and Jesus as Son. This writing will take us back to the original teachings of the New Testament. Jesus is the Son who will continue His Father's dynasty. He will rule until the kingdom of God is established on earth. This dynasty is the very kingdom we continue to advance in the name of Jesus.

I have heard it said that once you buy a car, like a silver Honda Accord, everywhere you go, you see silver Honda Accords. Whatever car you commit to, you see it everywhere, but before your purchase, you failed to notice any vehicles of this make and color.

In the same way, once I placed value upon the idea that there were two powers in heaven, I noticed it throughout the Bible. The principle is: whatever you commit to and place value upon, you see. I pray a blessing on your reading of "Are There Two Powers in Heaven?" May the words of Isaiah be reversed, and a good outcome is released, that all will **"...see with their eyes, and hear with their ears, and understand with their hearts, and turn and be healed"** (Isaiah 6:10 ESV).[3]

---

[3] Isaiah 6:9-10, the Lord tells Isaiah to preach **"Keep on hearing, but do not understand; keep on seeing, but do not perceive. Make the heart of this people dull, and their ears heavy, and blind their eyes."** Prior to the quote above it says, "lest they see...hear...understand."

Chapter Six

ROYAL SUCCESSION

...David(One deeply loved) will be like our God, like the Angel-
Yahweh(Messenger of the Jealous one)...
(Zechariah 12:8 TNT)

Mystery stirs the human heart to dig deeper into the unknown and to uncover hidden treasures that eyes have not yet seen. Mystery excites us to seek and find, creating holy adrenaline that fuels the soul's journey towards its destination. The journey you are about to embark on is uncovering the heartfelt narrative bound together in a book that humanity has received as a gift from the Creator. This book is called the Bible, the Greek word Biblia which means 'book.' This Holy Book is set apart above all other books because it is a message of a loving King and his Son.

The early church had deep roots in Jewish thought. The nation of Israel called their God by his name, Yahweh. The Jews who came to believe in Jesus saw Him as the other power and royal prince of heaven. Jesus was enthroned as a king who sat on the throne of His Father. The dynasty of Yahweh continues through his Son, Jesus.

The Old Testament conceals what New Testament reveals. The New Testament never reveals the name of the Father, and the Old Testament does not indicate the name of the Son. The Father and the Son are present throughout the Old and

17

New Testaments, and each can be more fully understood as we unpack their appearances.

Jesus is the eternal Son of God and the name which saves us. His name in Hebrew means "Yahweh will save," and Jesus is our door to the kingdom.

For there is salvation in no one else, for there is no other name under heaven that is given to man by which we must be saved (Acts 4:12 NIV).

Jesus is everything His Father is, but He is not Yahweh. The Bible distinguishes between the Father and the Son, though there is only one throne on which the Father and Son reign.

Yahweh and His Son, Jesus, are the two powers in heaven, and the Spirit is their breath, or life, that comes upon us and in us. The Spirit is not a separate person with a distinct personality. But instead, the Spirit is the person of Yahweh or the person of Jesus.

The New Testament begins with the declaration that there is a Son of the God of the Old Testament. In his gospel, Mark declares, **"...the beginning of the good news about Jesus, the Messiah, the Son of God..."** (Mark 1:1). The Old Testament ends with the warning of a curse.

"He will restore the hearts of the fathers to their children and the hearts of the children to their fathers, so that I will not come and smite the land with a curse" (Malachi 4:6 NAS).

A destructive curse is released because of the lack of heart connection between fathers and their children. As we finish the New Testament, we understand there is no more curse.

The most prevalent and destructive curse that exists is the curse of fatherlessness. Jesus, the Son of God, sits on the throne at the right hand of His Father and has broken this curse forever. The New Testament ends with a picture of a two-seated throne descending from heaven. John writes:

"No longer will there be any curse. The throne of God and of the Lamb will be in the city…" (Revelation 22:3 NIV).

How many powers exist in heaven? Is there one power, two powers, or three powers? This writing exists because of the tension I discovered between what I was told to believe and what was written in the Scriptures.

IMAGINE IN ANCIENT TIMES, A KINGDOM UNDER THE RULE OF A RIGHTEOUS, POWERFUL RULER. IMAGINE THE JOY OF THE PEOPLE IN THIS KINGDOM RESTING IN A STABLE EMPIRE. BUT AS THE YEARS GO BY, THE KING FAILS TO PRODUCE A MALE OFFSPRING. AND IF YOU KNOW ANYTHING ABOUT KINGDOMS, ONCE THE KING DIES, THE KINGDOM GOES INTO TURMOIL WITHOUT A MALE HEIR.

Chapter Seven

ANOTHER POWER?

When Jesus arrived on the planet, many Jews believed that Jesus was the Messiah, the other power of heaven coming to earth. Yet, most Jewish leaders did not accept Jesus as the one who fulfilled that role.

When the Jewish temple was destroyed in 70 A.D., the Jewish sect of the Pharisees continued guiding the spiritual direction of the Jewish people scattered in synagogues all over the Roman empire. They decided to abandon the idea of two powers in heaven and emphasize monotheism, or the belief in only one power in heaven. This shift was a reaction to the success of Christianity in the Roman empire.

Why do I believe this scenario? Because Jesus was so readily worshipped and honored in the same manner as Yahweh was. If the Jewish people, in the time of Jesus, were strict monotheists, the early Jewish Christians would have rejected the idea of honoring Jesus in the same way that Yahweh was honored.

Furthermore, Jews began to accuse Christians of being polytheists or believers in multiple gods. The Greeks practiced polytheism. Many Christians felt labeled as following the teaching of Plato and Socrates instead of the teachings of Moses and the prophets. As Christian theologians began to debate Jews, this accusation continued.

As years passed, Christians began to assume that the Jews, in the times of Jesus, were strict monotheists instead of believers in two powers in heaven. Later, Christians began using the idea of the Trinity, which included the person of the Holy Spirit. They taught the idea that God was one God who exists in three persons.

Many Jews who refused to accept Jesus as the Messiah used the concept of monotheism to exclude the role Jesus claimed to fulfill. Followers of Jesus were said to believe in two gods and be polytheists like the heathens. This accusation caused Christians to react to a lie instead of responding to the truth.

The church's theology in the 4th century refuted the accusation of polytheism by using the concept of the Trinity. When searching the New Testament, you will never find the word "Trinity," nor did disciples of Jesus use the Trinity as a defense against the Jews who did not believe in Jesus. The first disciples of Jesus understood the Jewish concept of the two powers in heaven.

THE WORD TRINITY IS NOT FOUND IN THE BIBLE, NOR IS IT EASILY UNDERSTOOD. THE TRINITY MUST BE TAUGHT AS A MYSTERY AND TO BE ACCEPTED BY FAITH.

Chapter Eight

DABAR YAHWEH

Most scholars would agree that Jesus is the Word in the gospel of John. The book of 1 Samuel tells us that Yahweh revealed himself by the word to Samuel. Many times in the Old Testament, we read that the word of Yahweh came to a prophet. The phrase "the word of Yahweh came" is quoted thirty-eight times alone in the book of Jeremiah. Every prophetic message Jeremiah received came from Dabar-Yahweh or the word-Yahweh.

The Hebrew word *dabar* is translated 85 different ways in the KJV. The word can mean a word or a thing. It is the word used to describe the ten commandments. *Dabar* in Hebrew is the word in spoken form and is the word in action. Hebraic thought includes the idea of movement when they speak of the word. It accomplishes something. The Word is not lifeless but living and active in the Hebrew mindset.

"The word of the LORD came" is a defining Biblical statement from a God who reveals Himself and expresses a deed to be accomplished. Young Samuel did not realize the voice of Yahweh because the Dabar-Yahweh was not yet revealed to him.

Now Samuel did not yet know Yawheh, and the word of Yahweh(*Dabar-Yahweh*) had not yet been revealed to him.

(1 Samuel 3:7 WEB)

22

Jesus is just like His Father. The word of Yahweh is fully revealed in the person of Jesus. Samuel could not know Yahweh unless the Word was shown to him. Jesus urges His disciples to get to know Him. Knowing Jesus is knowing the Father.

No one comes to the Father, except through me. If you had known me, you would have known my Father also. From now on, you know him, and have seen him. (John 14:6-7 WEB) Phillip, the disciple of Jesus responds, **"Lord, show us the Father, and that will be enough for us"** (vs. 8). We can know the Father because the Son is revealed to us. Jesus answers Phillip: **"He who has seen me has seen the Father"** (vs. 9). The Word of Yahweh allows the Yahweh to be revealed to us. We can see this pattern also in the life of Samuel.

Yahweh appeared again in Shiloh; for Yahweh revealed himself to Samuel in Shiloh by the word of Yahweh.

(1 Samuel 3:21 WEB)

The first verse of the gospel of John shows us the centrality of the Word of God in our theology. Yet most translations of John 1:1 do not present two powers but instead act as if Jesus is both with God and is God.

In the beginning was the Word, and the Word was with God, and the Word was God. (John 1:1 ESV)

The next question would be, "How can someone be with God and be God?" The concept of the Trinity was created to answer such a question. In the mind of those who formulated the Trinity, Yahweh, Jesus, and the Holy Spirit were made of God substance, and humankind was made of a man substance. These ideas were rooted in Greek philosophy instead of Biblical theology. The accurate translation of this Scripture is as follows:

In the beginning the Word was with the God and the Word was a God. (John 1:1)

Let me give you an example. The Bible points us to another power in heaven beside God Himself. Yahweh gave His Son all authority on heaven and earth. Translators dropped the article 'a' in front of God, and we read God as a name instead of a title.

The best way to translate the word "God" is to use it the same way you would use the title "King." The word king is a title we would give someone who rules. David was a king and was called "King David." David is his name, and King is his title. Throughout the Old Testament, Yahweh was a God, and He was called God Yahweh. God was His title, and Yahweh was His name. Yahweh is designated as the Most High God. Let me reword John 1:1, substituting the title of 'King' instead of the title of 'God.'

In the beginning was the Word, and the Word was with the King, and the Word was a King (John 1:1).

John 1:1 makes sense when we designate the word "God" as a title. Translating God without definite articles (i.e., the) and indefinite articles (i.e., a) creates confusion in a simple statement. Our translations steer the reader in a specific direction toward a particular goal. Understanding Jesus as the second power in heaven is a powerful revelation foretold throughout the Bible.

Most theological schools teach that a special grammatical rule for John 1:1 allows the translation to drop the 'a' before God.

If we understood that God is a title, not a name, the Scripture would not need to be inaccurately translated.

The early Christians were part of the Jewish community but were excommunicated because they elevated Jesus as the second power in heaven. They were not accused of believing in three powers in heaven– only two.

Most Christians before 70 A.D. attended the synagogue alongside other Jews who did not accept Jesus as the Messiah. Rabbis even began to develop recitations for the synagogue service in hopes of offending those who had trusted Jesus as their Savior. Early accusations against Christians by the rabbis claimed they were involved in the "two power heresy." The parents of the man born blind that was healed by Jesus vaguely responded to the Pharisees because they feared being excommunicated.

His parents said these things because they feared the Jews, for the Jews had already agreed that if anyone should confess Jesus to be Christ, he was to be put out of the synagogue.

(John 9:22 ESV)

The "two power heretics" were excommunicated and even killed by those in Jewish leadership. Christians were labeled as blasphemers because they considered Jesus the other power in heaven. The affirmation of truth for every Christian is that the Father and a Son rule on the same throne.

Chapter Nine

COVENANT MAKER

After the thousand-year era, Jesus, jointly with the Father (Yahweh), governs together into eternity. In the Old Testament era, Yahweh ruled as King over heaven. In the New Testament era, Jesus extends heaven's rule to earth through His disciples by His Spirit. He then physically returns to earth to rule during the millennium.

Covenants are agreements between two parties to solidify an ongoing relationship into the unknown future. The God of the universe is a covenant-making God. I have argued that the word *echad* in the Shema points to Yahweh being relational and desiring to make a covenant with humanity more than his numerical status. Yahweh is continually reaching out throughout history to secure a covenant relationship with humankind.

As he did with Adam and Noah, Yahweh reaches out to Abram to bring him into covenant, but he does this in a mysterious ceremony. First, he puts Abram into a deep sleep:

As the sun was going down, a deep sleep fell on Abram. And behold, dreadful and great darkness fell upon him. Then the Lord said to Abram, "Know for certain that your offspring will be sojourners in a land that is not theirs and will be servants there, and they will be afflicted for four hundred

years" (Genesis 15:12-13).

Deep supernatural sleep is defined as *"a state of divine revelation and activity."*[4] The Hebrew word *tardēmāh* is mentioned seven times in Scripture, including when Yahweh put Adam to sleep in the Garden of Eden. When Yahweh brought Abram into covenant, the ceremony involved a smoking fire pot and a flaming torch.

When the sun had gone down and it was dark, behold, a smoking fire pot and a flaming torch passed between these pieces. On that day, Yahweh made a covenant with Abram.

(Genesis 15:17-18 WEB)

During an ancient covenantal ceremony, each covenant partner cuts an animal into two pieces and walks between the animal carcasses. Each covenant partner would declare, "May I become like this animal if I ever violate the terms of this covenant."

Two Parties Coming Into Covenant

An Ancient Covenant

An animal is cut in two and the parties walk between the pieces and declare "May this happen to me if I ever violate the terms of this covenant"

---

[4] Zodhiates, Spiros, and John R. Kohlenberger. *The Hebrew-Greek Key Study Bible: New International Version.* Chattanooga, TN: AMG Pub., 1996. 1659.

27

Whenever two people would walk between the pieces of the animal's carcass, it would form the number eight. Interestingly, the number eight(using the Western Arabic numeral system) is the shape made by those entering into a covenant. Eight is the number that signifies a new covenant beginning by cutting off from the past. On the eighth day, every Jewish boy was circumcised and brought into the covenant of Abraham, Isaac, and Jacob.

Yahweh, represented by the smoking fire pot, walked between the pieces as the representative of heaven. Jesus, represented by the flaming torch, took the place of Abram as the future representative of earth. This covenant that Yahweh made with Abram did not require Abram to walk between the pieces of the animal. Jesus would come to planet earth two thousand years later to fulfill his pledge to be torn apart as a man for the violations of humanity.

Missionary expert and author Don Richardson asks some questions concerning this story.

Why did God ordain two sources of light to emphasize the importance of a sacrifice for sin as a response to that dreadful darkness? And why was the first light source, the smoking firepot, so much dimmer than the second light source that followed, described as a blazing torch?[5]

The unveiling of Jesus is sensed on every smoking page of the Hebrew Bible! A smoking pot is a fire not yet revealed and

---

[5] Richardson, Don. Heaven Wins (p. 120). Baker Publishing Group. Kindle Edition.

is a picture of Jesus in the Old Testament. It is smoking with revelation and great expectation of soon bursting flames.

The torch is the bright and shining revelation of the Son of God Himself, blazing onto the pages of the New Testament. Jesus said in the gospel of John:

I am the light of the world. Whoever follows me will not walk in darkness, but will have the light of life (John 8:12 ESV).

Throughout the Bible, there is a precise plan that involves both Father and Son to see it accomplished– two powers in heaven.

COVENANT IS A SOLEMN CONTRACT, OATH, OR BOND BETWEEN TWO PARTIES. THE MOST POWERFUL COVENANT KNOWN TO MAN IS THAT BETWEEN A FATHER AND SON. THE SON IS THE ONE WHO WILL CONTINUE ON THE DYNASTY OF HIS FATHER. WHEN A SON CARRIES OUT THIS SOLEMN DUTY, THERE IS SOMETHING BEAUTIFUL RELEASED FROM HEAVEN TO EARTH.

29

Chapter Ten

BEHOLD A SON!

The first son of Jacob was named Rueben. In Hebrew, the name means "I see a son!" or "Behold a son!" The first tribe of Israel is a prophetic statement for all Jews to recognize Jesus as the Son of God who will bring their nation into the right relationship with Yahweh.

As we study the Old Testament, we will discover some great scriptures that will cause us to exclaim, "I see a son!" Unfortunately, many Jews who love the Old Testament were blinded to the idea that there is another power in Heaven named Jesus.

Historically, Jewish scholars failed to acknowledge Jesus as the rightful heir to the throne of Yahweh. Solomon wrote in Proverbs 30:4 a question about his God: "What is his name and the name of his son?"

Who has gone up to Heaven and come down? Whose hands have gathered up the wind? Who has wrapped up the waters in a cloak? Who has established all the ends of the earth? What is his name, and what is the name of his son? Surely you know! (Proverbs 30:4 NIV)

Many early rabbis even claimed Yahweh was angry with Solomon because of what he wrote in Proverbs 30:4. They claimed God said to Solomon, "Why do express a thing that concerns the sanctification of my name with by an obscure allusion?"[6] Why would Solomon refer to the name of the son of the One who controls nature? Was Solomon alluding to a Son who would soon sit on the throne of His Father?

This mystery unfolds throughout the Old Testament of the coming Son of Yahweh– the other power in Heaven whose name is Jesus. The Hebraic Scriptures point to a future where Yahweh appoints a Son to the throne–not just a man like you and me, but one who is like His Father in every way.

I want you to consider only using the Scriptures to develop your understanding of who our God is and who Jesus is. Five hundred years ago, Martin Luther, the father of Protestantism, proclaimed, "Sola Scriptura," which means that the Bible is the source of our belief system and is the center of our lives in determining the rules of faith. Later theology and writings cannot take precedence over the Scriptures.

On the testimony of two or three witnesses, a matter is established. **"Only on the evidence of two witnesses or of three witnesses shall a charge be established"** (Deuteronomy 19:15 ESV). One power would not be enough to establish a matter– two were needed. Jesus alone could not validate his claims unless he had another to confirm the issue. **It's also written in your law that the testimony of two people is valid. I am one who testifies about myself, and the Father who sent me testifies about me.** (John 8:17-18 ESV).

---

[6] Alan Segal, Two Powers in Heaven

Together, the Father and the Son agree and validate the truth of the claims of Jesus. The Two Power teaching is the most fluent understanding of Yahweh and Jesus and how they relate. This view has been lost as the church has defended that God is "Three in One," and the Jews have defended that God is "One and No More." A closer look into history reveals that the Ancient of Days and the Son of Man rule the universe from their thrones in Heaven.

THE SCALES FELL OFF SAUL'S EYES, AND WHAT DID HE PREACH? "IMMEDIATELY IN THE SYNAGOGUES HE PROCLAIMED THE CHRIST, THAT HE IS THE SON OF GOD. " (ACTS 9:20 ESV) . HOW DID THE MESSAGE OF THE GOSPEL BECOME SO COMPLICATED? THEOLOGICAL LANGUAGE HAS OFTEN OVERLOOKED THE MOST BASIC, SIMPLE, AND BEAUTIFUL MESSAGE; A FATHER WHO EMPOWERS A SON TO RULE IN HIS NAME, AND A SON WHO IS OBEDIENT TO FULFILL HIS FATHER'S WISHES. I EARNESTLY PRAY THAT THIS MESSAGE WILL BECOME THE CORE OF OUR THEOLOGY.

Chapter Eleven

SON OF MAN

There are subtle hints in Scripture of Yahweh having a divine Son who would rule in the authority of his father. Daniel Boyarin summarizes the dream of Daniel chapter 7 as follows:

(1) There are two thrones. "As I looked, thrones were placed" (Daniel 7:9).

(2) There are two divine figures, one apparently old and one apparently young.

(3) The young figure is to be the Redeemer and eternal ruler of the world.

Yet there are some Scriptures that clearly show us that there is another power in heaven. The concept of a second power in heaven is presented most clearly in the book of Daniel. In this book, there is a vision that describes "...**one like a son of man,**" who is "...**coming with the clouds.**"

In my vision at night I looked, and there before me was one like a son of man, coming with the clouds of heaven. He approached the Ancient of Days and was led into his presence. (Daniel 7:13 NIV)

To come on clouds in Ancient Near Eastern writing meant you were qualified to apply for the God position. The Psalmist declares Yahweh as the one who **"...makes the clouds his chariot; he rides on the wings of the wind"** (Psalm 104:3).[7]

This second power of heaven is also a cloud rider.[8]

...you will see the Son of Man sitting at the right hand of the Mighty One and coming on the clouds of heaven.

(Matthew 26:64; Mark 14:62)

Note that the response of the Jewish leadership was to accuse Jesus of blasphemy. Jewish leaders believed that the title of the Son of Man was as powerful as the title of God. Anyone declaring themselves to be the Son of Man claimed to be heaven's second power. Note the response of the high priest:

Then the high priest tore his robes and said, "He has uttered blasphemy. What further witnesses do we need? You have now heard his blasphemy." (Matthew 26:65 ESV)

The response of everyone on the council was to condemn Jesus to death. The Sanhedrin did not say, "Jesus is claiming to be Yahweh in the flesh!" Jesus was announcing himself as the Son of Man who sits on the throne of His Father.

And the high priest tore his garments and said, "What further witnesses do we need? You have heard his blasphemy. What

---

[7] Why is that a big deal? Because everywhere else that description occurs in the Old Testament, it was used only of God himself (Isa. 19:1; Deut. 33:26; Ps. 68:32–33; Ps. 104:1–4). Heiser, Michael S. Supernatural: What the Bible Teaches about the Unseen World And Why It Matters (p. 119). Lexham Press. Kindle Edition.

[8] "The act of coming with clouds suggests a theophany of Yahweh himself. If Dan. vii. 13 does not refer to a divine being, then it is the only exception out of about seventy passages in the O[ld] T[estament]." Boyarin, Daniel. The Jewish Gospels . The New Press. Kindle Edition.

is your decision?" And they all condemned him as deserving death. (Mark 14:63-64 ESV)

Early Jewish Christians could recognize Jesus as a second power different from Yahweh. Jesus embraced his position as the other power of heaven who comes alongside the Ancient of Days.

Jesus most often referred to himself as the Son of Man. The high priest responded harshly to Jesus' claim to this title because this claim was not true or false–it was true or blasphemous! His confession as the Son of Man brought Him the death penalty. This heavenly title is described in the vision of Daniel:

He was given authority, glory, and sovereign power; all peoples, nations and men of every language worshiped him. His dominion is an everlasting dominion that will not pass away, and his kingdom is one that will never be destroyed. (Daniel 7:14 NIV)

Jews in the time of Jesus understood the "one like the son of man" as another power in heaven. Yahweh was seated on his throne and called the "Ancient of Days." Jesus rode in on the clouds and was called "one like the son of man." One like the Son of Man was given authority, glory, and sovereign power, and all peoples and nations worshipped Him. This other figure is not the Ancient of Days, yet powerful and revered.

Ancient Jewish rabbis described the dream in Daniel chapter two as follows:

The younger one has his own throne (that's why there is more than one throne set up to start with), and he is invested by the older one

35

with dominion, glory, and kingship over all the peoples of the world; not only that, but it will be an eternal kingship forever and ever. This is the vision that will become in the fullness of time the story of the Father and the Son.[9]

A Father enthroning his Son over his kingdom was the Biblical narrative in Jesus' time. Rabbi Boyarin summarizes by saying, *"If Daniel is the prophecy, the Gospels are the fulfillment."*[10]

JESUS WAS MORE OF A MESSIAH THAN THE JEWS EXPECTED. THEY BELIEVED HE WOULD BE LIKE MOSES. INSTEAD, HE CAME DECLARING HIMSELF TO BE "THE SON OF GOD" AND "THE SON OF MAN." JESUS IS ONE WITH THE FATHER; THEREFORE, AS WE WORSHIP THE FATHER, WE ALSO WORSHIP THE SON. JESUS IS DOING THE WORK OF THE FATHER HERE ON EARTH AND WILL REIGN UNTIL EVERYTHING IS SUBJECTED TO HIS FATHER. ONCE HIS WORK IS COMPLETE, HE TOO, WILL SUBJECT HIMSELF TO THE FATHER, SO THAT GOD MAY BE ALL IN ALL.

---

[9] Boyarin, Daniel. The Jewish Gospels . The New Press. Kindle Edition.
[10] Ibid

Chapter Twelve

SON OF GOD

Most Christians assumed that the title "Son of God" inferred Jesus' heavenly identity, and the title "Son of Man" implied his connection to his humanity. Yet the opposite is true. Luke's genealogy ends with **"...the son of Enos, the son of Seth, the son of Adam, the son of God"** (Luke 3:38 ESV). Adam was considered a son of God. Matthew's genealogies go as far back as Abraham, but Luke's genealogies go back to Adam. To remember this fact, note that Matthew and Abraham have seven letters each, and Luke and Adam have four.

When Jesus was unjustly condemned to die, He identified Himself as the Son of man coming on the clouds. The "Son of Man" title is the heavenly title of Jesus, and the "Son of God" is the earthly title. Only someone like Yahweh could ride on the clouds. Jesus had cloud riding listed on His resume and refers to Himself under oath when questioned by the high priest:

The high priest said to him, "I charge you under oath by the living God: Tell us if you are the Christ, the Son of God." "Yes, it is as you say," Jesus replied. "But I say to all of you: In the future, you will see the Son of Man sitting at the right hand of the Mighty One and coming on the clouds of heaven." (Matthew 26:63-64 NIV)

37

Note that Jesus choices to call Himself the Son of Man. He connects himself to the one spoken of in the book of Daniel. Daniel had a vision and saw two powers in heaven. Cloud riders in ancient settings are those who can receive worship.

Daniel Boyarin writes: *"Jesus entered into a role that existed prior to his birth, and this is why so many Jews were prepared to accept him as the Christ, as the Messiah, Son of Man."*[11] Jesus identified as the "Son of Man" because his audience understood the implications of his statement.

The original arguments between Jews and Christians were not over a triune God but the other power of heaven. Rabbis dug their heels in on the issue of the oneness of God with the emphasis on His singularity. Christian theologians then overreacted to the polytheist label and embraced the philosophical device called the Trinity. This doctrine allowed Christianity to be understood as a monotheistic religion and still allowed Jesus to have a God license.

ECHAD IS USED TO SIGNIFY A UNION OR A JOINING TOGETHER IN COVENANT. WHEN 'ONE' IS REFERRED TO IN RELATIONSHIPS, IT POINTS TO A COVENANT, NOT A NUMBER.

---

[11] Boyarin, Daniel. The Jewish Gospels . The New Press. Kindle Edition.

Chapter Thirteen

THE NARRATIVE

A narrative is a basic storyline that we believe about a series of related events. Each of us has a narrative about the Bible that can either help us or hinder us from understanding what is written on its pages. A wrong narrative will impede our understanding. The Trinity is the narrative most Christians assume when approaching the concept of God. Still, this doctrine lacks the clear and straightforward Bible understanding of a King who passes on His authority and power to His chosen Son.

Nebuchadnezzar experienced the revelation of a God who had a son. As he cast three Hebrews into a burning furnace, he shouted:

"Look!" he answered, "I see four men loose, walking in the midst of the fire; and they are not hurt, and the form of the fourth is like the Son of God" (Daniel 3:25 NIV)

We should not be surprised about the fluidity of the narrative from the Old Testament to the New Testament. The Son of God was confirmed even by a pagan king who persecuted righteous Jews.

The Bible emphasizes the importance of a monarchy passing on the throne to a righteous son. A dynasty continues on into the future through godly offspring and establishes the kingdom from generation to generation.

39

King David made preparations for the Temple for his son Solomon to build. Solomon was the chosen predecessor of his father to sit on his throne. Yet the father and son had different roles when it came to establishing a Temple in Jerusalem.

David said to Solomon: "My son, I had it in my heart to build a house for the Name of the Lord my God. But this word of the Lord came to me: 'You have shed much blood and have fought many wars. You are not to build a house for my Name, because you have shed much blood on the earth in my sight. But you will have a son who will be a man of peace and rest, and I will give him rest from all his enemies on every side. His name will be Solomon, and I will grant Israel peace and quiet during his reign. (1 Chronicles 22:7-9 NIV)**

King David was not allowed to build the Temple, but his son Solomon was ordained for the task.

Yahweh made preparations for the kingdom of God to be established on Earth. And just like King David, God the Father prepares the way for the Son to fulfill his plan. First in the natural, then in the spiritual.

In the book of Leviticus, God is commanding the Israelites on how to make atonement for their sins. Atonement is the Hebrew word *kaphar*, which means to cover while inferring forgiveness or a release from debt. English translators created the word "at-one-ment" so that *kaphar* would suggest how to become one with God. Just like David did not take the role of being the one to build the Temple and establish the place of sacrifice, the high priest would pass that task on to his son. This principle carries on into the New Testament and Jesus's role as the Son of God.

In Leviticus 16, God is commanding the Israelites on how to make a blood sacrifice that would cover the sins of the people. Yahweh tells them to take two goats; one to slaughter and one to set free. Once this is completed, one goat is let go, and the other is sacrificed. The goat that is released is called the 'scapegoat.' At that time, Aaron, the high priest, is commanded to lay his hands on the scapegoat and confess the people's sins. But according to verse 32, it is the son who makes atonement for the people.

The priest who is anointed and ordained to succeed his father as high priest is to make atonement. He is to put on the sacred linen garments and make atonement for the Most Holy Place, for the tent of meeting and the altar, and for the priests and all the members of the community" (Leviticus 16:32-33) The high priest's son, ordained to succeed his father, would make the atonement. This same principle is found in the story of Abraham and Isaac. The father prepared the way for the son to be offered up as the sacrifice.

THE ANCIENTS UNDERSTOOD THE POWER OF A DYNASTY. THE SON DESERVED THE HONOR AND RESPECT IN THE SAME MANNER AS THE FATHER. ANYONE WHO DISPUTED THE RIGHTS OF THE SON TO THE THRONE WOULD NOT LIVE A LONG LIFE!

Chapter Fourteen

LOVE SACRIFICE

Abraham climbed Mount Moriah to sacrifice his one and only son foreshadowing of what Jesus would later do. This act is called the 'Alkedah' in Jewish tradition or the binding of Isaac, which is seen as the event which is the pinnacle of all Jewish history. Note that the words of Jesus in John 3:16 are also the pinnacle of the entire New Testament revelation:

For God so loved the world, that he gave his only Son, that whoever believes in him should not perish but have eternal life. (John 3:16 ESV)

For God so loved the world that he gave his only Son. The word "only" is often translated as "only begotten," which infers only born. The word for 'only' in John 3:16 in the Greek language is *monogenes*. Jesus is not an onlyborn son but instead the unique son who sits on the throne of Yahweh. The same Greek word is used in the book of Hebrews to describe Isaac– Abraham's only(*monogenes*) son:

By faith Abraham, when he was tested, offered up Isaac, and he who had received the promises was in the act of offering up his only(*monogenes*) son. (Hebrews 11:17 ESV)

We know that Isaac was not the only son of Abraham. He had another son named Ishmael. Isaac was not the onlyborn son of Abraham–- he was the unique son of the promise. Genesis 22:2

says, **"Take your son, your only son Isaac, whom you love."** It is the first time that love is mentioned in the Bible and describes the heart-wrenching love of a Father giving up his precious son to die.

Like Yahweh established a covenant with Abram, he founded another covenant for you and me two thousand years ago. Jesus came as a man, and because the covenant was violated, he was torn into pieces as the sacrifice for every covenant breaker.

The Hebrew Bible describes the agony of Abraham sacrificing his only son, the one whom he loved, to the LORD. John 3:16 echoes this sacrifice. The first mention of love is mentioned in this story in Genesis 22, as Yahweh commands Abraham:

Take your son, your only son Isaac, whom you love, and go to the land of Moriah, and offer him there as a burnt offering on one of the mountains of which I shall tell you.

(Genesis 22:2 ESV).

The lesser-known sacrifice of Hannah, the mother of Samuel, is also noteworthy. Hannah was barren but prayed and was given a son whom she later dedicated to the Temple. She gave up her only son once he was weaned to fulfill her promise to Yahweh. She declared:

Those who strive with Yahweh(*Jealous one***) will be broken to pieces. He will thunder against them in the sky.**

Yahweh(*Jealous one***) will judge the ends of the earth. He will**

give strength to his king, and exalt the horn of his anointed.

(1 Samuel 2:10 TNT).

Interestingly, Hannah asks for the king to receive strength and the anointed to be exalted. Since there was no king until after her son Samuel was older, was she prophesying about the future Messiah King?

Yahweh's plan allowed his Son to become the sacrifice for the sins of the world sins and be the ultimate expression of love for all humanity to see. When we look at the gift the Father gave us, what more could we ask for than his only Son? As Paul wrote to the Roman church:

He who did not spare his own Son but gave him up for us all, how will he not also with him graciously give us all things?

(Romans 8:32 ESV)

Jesus was not sent to convince us that we were sinners. Jesus was sent to convince us of our worth to our God, which is the New Testament's good news. Yahweh would give up His Son for the sins of all humankind.

The Son is the radiance of God's glory and the exact representation of his being, sustaining all things by his powerful word. After he had provided purification for sins, he sat down at the right hand of the Majesty in heaven.

(Hebrew 1:3 NIV)

"THIS IS MY SON, WHOM I LOVE" (MATTHEW 3:17) .

Chapter Fifteen

SON SUCCESSION

Every king sought to have his kingdom continue after his death through a faithful son. 2 Esdras, an ancient Jewish writing from the 2nd Century A.D. describes a heavenly figure who appears to be God's Son.

Esdras saw upon the mount Sion a great people, whom I could not number, and they all praised the Lord with songs. And in the midst of them, there was a young man of a high stature, taller than all the rest, and upon every one of their heads he set crowns, and was more exalted, which I marveled at greatly. So, I asked the angel, and said, Sir, what are these? He answered and said unto me, These be they that have put off the mortal clothing, and put on the immortal, and have confessed the name of God: now are they crowned, and receive palms. Then said I unto the angel, What young person is it that crowned them, and giveth them palms in their hands? So, he answered and said unto me, It is the Son of God, whom they have confessed in the world. Then began I greatly to commend them that stood so stiffly for the name of the Lord. (2 Esdras 2:42)

The Son of God is the second power of heaven and is everything his Father is. The Father delegates all his authority to rule to his eternal Son- this is the straightforward narrative of the Bible that Jews in the time of Jesus understood.

Jacob named his first son Rueben. I believe seeing the son, as the name Rueben means, is the first step. As we go through the rest of the name meanings of Jacob's sons, we see our journey as a Christian.

Name	Meaning
Rueben	"I see a son!"
Simeon	"I heard and obeyed"
Levi	"Attached"
Judah	"Praise"
Dan	"Judge"
Naphtali	"My struggle"
Gad	"Fortunate"
Asher	"Happy"
Issachar	"Hired for wage"
Zebulun	"Glorious dwelling"
Joseph	"May He add"
Benjamin	"Son of my right hand"

The revelation of the Son, Jesus Christ, unfolded from beginning of the book of Genesis to the end of the book of Revelation. Jesus was revealed as a son but now is being declared by the Father, as a son of my right hand.

Chapter Sixteen

MONOTHEISM

Houston, we have a problem! We have Jesus praying to His Father in heaven. If there is only one God, then we must all become monotheists. If we are all monotheists and Jesus is praying to the God of heaven, we have a problem. Where does Jesus fit into monotheism?

Monotheism is defined as the belief in one God. Though Yahweh never states, "You shall be monotheistic," the concept became the central doctrinal belief for every Jew. Since Christianity was a seed planted in the soil of Biblical Judaism, the sacredness of monotheism continues to be a central teaching of Christians.

Let us study the teachings of Jesus and the apostles from a Jewish mindset. Most Jewish people believe in one God named Yahweh, but they do not accept that Jesus was His Son. The Jews would react to any second power in heaven with the accusation of heresy and a denial based upon the sacredness of monotheism. Even Jesus Himself was asked about the most important commandment. He responded by saying: **The most important is, 'Hear, O Israel: The Lord our God, the Lord is one'** (Mark 12:29 ESV).

Yahweh is the name of the God of the Old Testament. On our journey to better understand the Bible, we must identify

Yahweh as the Father of Jesus and Jesus as the unique son of Yahweh. There is no need to see this relationship in any other manner than a Father-Son relationship. As we focus on this relationship, both the Old and New Testaments will begin to come into focus.

Almost all modern translations exchange the name of Yahweh for the title "LORD." The four letters that make up this name, YHWH, are called the Tetragrammaton. 'Yahweh' is the most common way to pronounce the Tetragrammaton, yet others have used 'Jehovah' or 'Yehovah.'

The Name Translation Bible is a project I have published that translates every name with its meaning next to it. In the TNT(The Name Translation) Bible, I translate Yahweh as a name, not a title. Using the name of Yahweh is offensive to many of my Jewish readers because of the tradition that forbids them to write or say his name.

I have not found any convincing reason to forbid the writing or the speaking of the name of Yahweh. His name is written over 6,000 times in the Scriptures, and I believe we should translate and speak what is written. Remember that Jesus told the religious leaders of His day, **"You have a fine way of rejecting the commandment of God in order to establish your tradition!"** (Mark 7:9 ESV). The word of God trumps tradition.

But one valid argument against the use of the name of Yahweh is its absence in the New Testament. When any Biblical text lacks Yahweh's name, it is easier to lose the distinction between the Father and the Son.[12] The gospel of Matthew is believed by many scholars to have been originally written in the Hebrew language and to have included the name of Yahweh.[13]

The Babylonian Talmud is an ancient Jewish writing that describes the dilemma of destroying Christian writings by fire even though the name of Yahweh is written in their pages. The rabbis argue over what should be done, even suggesting cutting out the divine name prior to their incineration.[14] Though the New Testament never uses the name of Yahweh, is it possible that it was included in the earliest manuscripts? The Babylonian Talmud seems to suggest this possibility.

NOW AN INTERMEDIARY IMPLIES MORE THAN ONE, BUT GOD IS ONE. (GALATIANS 3:20 ESV)

---

[12] It was they who demanded, in effect, that Christianity be "updated" by blurring or even obliterating the long-accepted distinction between the Father and the Son. Rubenstein, Richard E. When Jesus Became God: The Epic Fight over Christ's Divinity in the Last Days of Rome (p. 74). Houghton Mifflin Harcourt. Kindle Edition.

[13] "Matthew put together the oracles [of the Lord] in the Hebrew language." (*The Ante-Nicene Fathers,* Vol. I, p. 155) Origen (184-253 A.D.) tells us that Matthew's Gospel was "published for Jewish believers, and composed in Hebrew letters." (M'Clintock and Strong's *Cyclopædia,* Vol. 5, p. 890) Eusebius (260-340 A.D.) states: "The evangelist Matthew delivered his Gospel in the Hebrew tongue."

[14] A famous rabbinic passage (Talmud Shabbat 13.5) discusses the problem of destroying heretical texts (very probably including books of Jewish-Christians).

Chapter Seventeen

THE TITLE OF GOD

Most translations do not allow the reader the option to quickly see that the God of the Old Testament had a name. Calling someone by their title is a sign of respect, but calling someone by their name is an invitation to greater intimacy. Some believe early translations of the Bible always included the written name of God (YHWH) and later translators chose to replace it with a title (LORD). This choice was most likely an uninformed decision to honor Jewish influences, but the consequences created more significant confusion.[15]

The TNT Bible also differentiates between titles and names, unlike other translations. God is a title, not a name. Yet, in most English translations, we say, "For God so loved the world," when we should say, "For the God so loved the world." The TNT translates John 3:16 as, "For our God so loved the world," because the more accurate translation as "the God" is hard to swallow and clunky sounding for most readers.

---

[15] "The removal of the Tetragrammaton (Jehovah) from the New Testament and its replacement with the surrogates KYRIOS and THEOS blurred the original distinction between the Lord God and the Lord Christ, and in many passages made it impossible which one was meant. As time went on…it was often impossible to distinguish between them. Thus, it may be that the removal of the Tetragrammaton (Jehovah) contributed significantly to the later…Trinity " – George Howard, Bible Scholar ; The Name of God in the New Testament, BAR 4.1 (March 1978), pg 15

The only time you find Yahweh given a name other than the four-letter Tetragrammaton is located in the book of Exodus. **"Do not worship any other god, for Yahweh, whose name is Jealous, is a jealous God"** (Exodus 34:14 TNT). Some scholars believe that the name Yahweh originates in the land of Midian and is derived from the Arabic term for *"desire, love or passion."*[16] I translated the name of Yahweh to mean "Jealous one" primarily because of the numerous Biblical declarations where Yahweh identifies with the emotion of jealousy. When you understand who someone is, you better understand their actions. In today's society, jealousy is one of the most embarrassing emotions to be accused of. This accusation usually points to someone insecure, vulnerable, and desperate. Yet in the Scriptures, we find our God, Yahweh, declaring, "I am a Jealous God!" Jealously is used to express a strong emotion toward one's possession. Yahweh jealousy possesses us and requires us to be entirely devoted to him.

The word for jealous in Hebrew is closely connected to the word qana. Qana *"...represents the act of the advancement of God and His glory over all substitutes."* The LORD (Yahweh) permits no rivals, and He is jealous for you and me. The nature of Yahweh is to be jealous for us to be utterly obedient to him and have no other gods before him.

---

[16] Shelomo Dov Goitein (1900-1985), a scholar of both Jewish and Arabic studies, suggested that the name derives from the Arabic root h.w.y and the word hawaya, which means "love, affection, passion, desire."

The goal of this writing is to restore the centrality of Jesus in our theology and our practice. But for many Christians, the Holy Spirit has taken the central place. Others have given Yahweh his rightful place but fail to provide Jesus with his place of honor.

The very idea of challenging the concept of monotheism may seem extreme. I have spent thousands of hours dividing that which is in God's Word from that which is based on man's doctrine. Is strict monotheism a central doctrine we must embrace as Christians? Yes, there is one God, Yahweh, and there is one Lord, Jesus. "God" and "Lord" are titles for both the Father and the Son, but both are to receive equal honor.

Paul writes within the first three decades after the death of Jesus and the birth of the church:

There is but one God, the Father, from whom all things came and for whom we live; and there is but one Lord, Jesus Christ, through whom all things came and through whom we live.

(1 Corinthians 8:6 ESV)

Paul summarizes: There is one God and one Lord. One plus one equals two. Jesus is the other power in heaven. The concept of strict monotheism allows only one central figure to be worshipped in its religion. As Christianity spread rapidly, Judaism embraced strict monotheism– hoping to exclude Jesus from his rightful place of worship. Before Jesus, Judaism fully expected a soon coming second power who would be the Messiah. If we embrace strict monotheism the way most theologians do today, we will have a more challenging time

52

putting Jesus in his proper position. When we accept the concept of two powers in heaven, Jesus now has his rightful place.

Yahweh's ten qualities

1. **Compassionate.** (Exodus 34:6, Jonah 4:2, Nehemiah 9:17, Psalm 86:15; 103:8 ;145:8)

2. **Gracious.** (Exodus 34:6, Jonah 4:2, Nehemiah 9:17, Psalm 86:15; 103:8 ;145:8)

3. **Forgiving.** (Nehemiah 9:17)

4. **Does not leave the guilty unpunished.** (Nahum 1:3)

5. **Slow to anger.** (Exodus 34:6; Jonah 4:2; Nehemiah 9:17; Psalm 145:8, Nahum 1:3)

6. **Abounding(rich) in love.** (Exodus 34:6; Jonah 4:2 Nehemiah 9:17; Psalm 86:15; 103:8 ;145:8)

7. **Abounding in faithfulness** (Exodus 34:6; Psalm 86:15)

8. **Relents from sending calamity.** (Jonah 4:2)

9. **Great in power.** (Nahum 1:3)

10. **Takes no bribes.** (Deuteronomy 10:17)

Chapter Eighteen

STRICT MONOTHEISM

Is true Christianity strictly monotheistic? Determining what a Christian should uphold as the basic tenants of faith must be firmly rooted in the Hebraic Scriptures (Old Testament). When we read the New Testament through the lenses of the Old Testament, we will receive not only information but revelation. Knowledge feeds the mind, but conviction is the goal. Having conviction about what you believe will change your life. Knowledge without conviction will only lead to pride and arguments.

The central cry of Judaism is Deuteronomy 6:4, **"Hear, O Israel, the LORD is God, the LORD is one."** This verse is often interpreted and understood to be a doctrinal declaration of strict, unitarian monotheism, expressing the belief that God exists as a strictly singular "oneness." But I believe this idea was emphasized amongst 1st Century Jews to alienate Christians and discredit the Lordship of Jesus Christ. Rabbis began to emphasize this verse because of the claims of Jesus Christ. Prior to the influence of Christianity, the idea that two powers in heaven existed was very common.

Since the spread of Christianity, the most important verse in the Bible to the Jewish people was Deuteronomy 6:4. This verse in the Hebrew language is so important that it has earned the title "The Shema." Shema in Hebrew means "to hear and obey." This Scripture is to the Jew what John 3:16 is to the Christian. Famous Jews throughout history have spoken the "Shema" in their last breath. It was a defiant cry that made them different from the pantheistic religions that surrounded them. Viewing God as "one" for the Jew is a sacred duty.

Rabbis throughout the centuries have emphasized the singularity of God in the "Shema." I believe the real Biblical emphasis is not His singularity but rather His desire for covenant. "One" in Hebraic thought denotes being together in covenant. We must keep this in mind when forming our theology.

What if the oneness of God or monotheism was not a theological emphasis when Jesus landed on this planet? The premise is that the Jews were quite comfortable in their theology with the role Jesus claimed. Only after the spread of Christianity did Jewish theology shift to a strict sort of monotheism.

The Jews accepted the role Jesus was claiming to fulfill, but most of the Jews did not receive Jesus as the one who was to fulfill that role. After the death and resurrection of Jesus, his acceptance as the "Son of Man" blossomed and forced a shift of emphasis in Jewish theology at that time. Once the Jewish temple was destroyed in 70 A.D., rabbis completely distanced themselves from the "two power" idea because of Jesus' claims as the Messiah.

Chapter Nineteen

ECHAD

The word for "one" in "the Shema" is the Hebrew word echad, which means united, one, alike, alone, altogether. "The Shema" is placed in the context of the Ten Commandments (or words) from Yahweh to His people. Following this verse is the Scripture urging them to:

"Love the Yahweh your God with all your heart, with all your soul, with all your mind, and with all your strength"
(Deuteronomy 6:5 NIV84).

Echad is used to signify a union or a joining together in covenant. When 'one' is referred to in relationships, it points to a covenant, not a number. Yahweh was telling His people that He is a covenant-making God, not that He was singular! This is why the "Shema" is found right in the midst of Yahweh's covenant promise. Take, for instance, the following Scripture in Genesis regarding man and woman becoming echad.

"For this reason, a man will leave his father and mother and be united to his wife, and they will become one flesh."
(Genesis 2:24).

When I got married, I became one flesh with my wife, yet we did not cease to exist as individuals. We share my last name, but we continue as separate people. We did not join our first names together to metamorphose into some indefinable mass.

Nor after we were married was it suitable now to refer to me as either my name or her name. *Echad* meant we became one in covenant– a commitment we made together to be together.

The Shema reminds us that Yahweh is reaching out to us to come into a relationship with Him. The Shema is an invitation to experience covenant with God Himself. The Jew claims the Shema points us to a monotheistic faith. I say the Shema points us to a God with His arms wide open to us.

Jews and Muslims alike contend there is only one God. I contend there is another power represented in heaven. I contend that this power should be honored in the same way that God Himself is honored. This second power in heaven is His Son, Jesus. To claim that God is one is to claim that He is a God who desires to make a covenant with you and me.

Islam especially treats the God of creation as a God of power. The emphasis on His greatness strikes great fear in the followers of Islam. Our God is not only a God of power, but more importantly, He is a God of empowerment. Empowerment can only happen in the context of a covenant. "Allah Akbar" means that "God is great!" Islam teaches that God is great, but Christianity also teaches that our God wants us to be great as well.

OUR GOD IS NOT JUST A GOD OF POWER– HE IS A GOD OF EMPOWERMENT!

Chapter Twenty

NO OTHER GODS

In the book of Isaiah, we read over and over that "There is no one like Yahweh" and "There is no God besides Him!" Though these statements direct us to a monotheistic conclusion, these statements can also be understood in a different light.

The Bible uses expressions that we sometimes should not take literally. If I tell my wife, "Honey, besides you, there is no other," I am telling her that I am loyal to her and to her only. She does not think I have lost my mind and now believes that she is the only person that exists. Deuteronomy 4:35 expresses, **"Yahweh is God; besides him, there is no other."** In light of the Son of God manifesting on earth, we should not take these statements to mean Jesus could not receive the title "God" along with Yahweh.

Imagine, after visiting the Statue of Liberty and the Empire State Building, my friend stated, "There is no place like New York City!" Did my friend really believe that New York City was the only place that existed? Would he argue with me if I claimed that I believed there were other cities in the world? The statement he is making is placing New York City as the city of all cities. He is saying that there is no other city in comparison to New York City and not that he believes New York City is the only city in existence.

Yahweh warns of the coming destruction of the city of Babylon, who personified says, **"I am, and there is no one besides me"** (Isaiah 47:8). The claim is not that Babylon is the only city in the world but instead that she has no rival. This is an expression of incomparability. The book of Isaiah makes many declarations.

"Is there any God besides me? No, there is no other Rock; I know not one" (Isaiah 44:8; 45:5,22; 46:9; 47:8,10).

Most scholars believe these statements of Yahweh are about declaring His preeminence above the gods of the nations. Unfortunately, these statements have been interpreted as an ultimatum in Scripture, forcing theologians to develop a doctrine of strict monotheism.

The first sentence in Genesis 1:1 states **"...God created...."** The Hebrew noun *Elohim* is plural, but the verb for create, *bara*, is singular. The plural *Elohim* leaves many to believe that God is hinting that He is more than one. However, there are other explanations for the use *of Elohim* (i.e., God plural) in the Scriptures. For example, plurality in the Hebrew language is sometimes used to emphasize or magnify. The grammar of ancient languages does not always follow the rules of the English language.

The English word 'trees' refer to more than one tree, while in Hebrew, the plural word for 'trees' is *etsiym* can refer to either more than one tree or one very large tree. *Behemoth* is the plural form of *behemah*, meaning beast, but it can refer to a very large beast or more than one beast. Using the word *Elohim* does not necessarily mean that there is a triune God, nor does it exclude the idea. Hebrew plurals allow the reader to see multiple gods or one big God.

Ecclesiastes 12:1 is most often translated as, **"Remember thy Creator in the days of thy youth."** But it should be rendered as, "Remember thy Creators." In Job 35:10, the actual translation should read, **"Where is our God, my Makers?"** Again, we read in Psalm 149:2, **"Let Israel rejoice in his Makers."** Is the pluralization of these Hebrew words to emphasize greatness, or is there a subtle inference to another creator standing beside Yahweh? Proverbs tells us, **"The knowledge of the Holy Ones is understanding"** (Proverbs 9:10), and Isaiah says, **"Your Makers are your husband"** (Isaiah 54:5).

These strange plural words might emphasize the enormity of our God as our Creator and Maker, or is something else being inferred? Is the Son of God included as one of our Makers and Creators?

PLURALITY IN ONE LANGUAGE DOES NOT NECESSARILY MEAN THE SAME THING IN EVERY LANGUAGE. THE 'WE' OF MAJESTY DOES NOT EXIST IN HEBREW.[17]

---

[17] Paul Joüon and Takamitsu Muraoka, *A Grammar of Biblical Hebrew* (vol. 2; Pontificio Istituto Biblico, 2003), 375–376 (Par. 114.e).

Chapter Twenty-One

YAHWEH ≠ TRINITY

Because of the monotheistic statements found in the book of Isaiah, many scholars teach that Yahweh is the Trinity. I disagree with this statement because Yahweh is the name of the Father of the Old Testament. We must not confuse His sacred name with that of His Son Jesus.

Most theologians teach that there are many names for the God of the Bible. Though Yahweh and Jesus assume many different titles, Yahweh and Jesus each have only one personal name. Yahweh, whose name means "Jealous one," is the Father of Jesus. Jesus, whose name means "Yahweh will save," is the son of Yahweh.

Our God has one name: Yahweh. His name is four letters in Hebrew, YHVH, which most Jews refuse to say because His Name is considered sacred. Most often, the name 'Yahweh' was translated as LORD (All Capital Letters). Our Jewish brethren felt it was honoring to keep the name of Yahweh sacred by not saying His name. In the TNT version, I chose to use the name of Yahweh though many readers are uncomfortable with the change. I believe His name is important to be included in the text, and excluding the name of Yahweh is a hindrance to good theology.

If His name was too sacred to speak or to translate, how come the Bible uses his shorter name or nickname, "Yah?" Every time we say, "Hallelujah," we are saying, "Praise You, Yah!" I do not believe Yahweh wanted his name hidden or unspoken. The ancient Jew of the Bible probably spoke the name of Yahweh as much as today's Christian speaks the name of Jesus.

Psalm 110:1 is the most quoted Old Testament scripture in the New Testament. Jesus used Psalm 110 to convince His Jewish brethren of who He was. Other New Testament authors often alluded to its content as well when pointing to who Jesus actually is. **"Yahweh says to my Lord, "Sit at my right hand until I make your enemies your footstool for your feet"** (Psalm 110:1 WEB)

In the New Testament, we find Jesus assuming the title of Lord. This title is key in understanding Psalm 110:1. The word in Hebrew for Lord (not all capitalized letters) is *Adonai* or *Adon*. This is the actual word in Hebrew for Lord and points most often to the person of Jesus.

Translating Psalm 110:1 from the perspective of a 1st Century Jew, it would most likely be understood as, **"Yahweh (The LORD) says to Jesus, (my Lord) sit at my right hand until I (Yahweh) make our enemies a footstool for your feet."** To turn the name of Yahweh into a triune being is nonsensical.

To say Yahweh is the Trinity is to imply that the Father, Son, and Spirit are all talking to the Son. No, Yahweh is speaking to his Son to sit at His right hand. Yahweh is elevating His Son to the highest place of honor– to sit at His right hand.

As Christians, we must be as Biblically accurate with our understanding of our God as possible. Let us take the mystery out of 'who Jesus is' and 'who our God is.' We need to present the truth in simplicity and with clarity: Jesus is the Son of God who is ruling the throne of Yahweh, his Father. The gospel says that Yahweh gave up His Son. How much easier is it to relate to this message: a Father who loves His Son and gives Him up for us, and the Son willingly giving up His life so that we might be saved?

Many Christians have great difficulty approaching God because they have relational problems with their earthly father. Once this father perspective is corrected, their connection to God is restored. Honoring earthly fathers and mothers is one of the most important commands given to us to follow.

'Honor your father and mother'—which is the first commandment with a promise— 'that it may go well with you and that you may enjoy long life on the earth.'
(Ephesians 6:2-3 NIV)

Honor releases us into a long life! We must honor those our God calls us to honor. When we honor Jesus, we are honoring the Father. Honoring Jesus brings pleasure to the Father and gives us access to enjoy a long life.

The Jewish establishment in the times of Jesus was expecting another power from heaven. There was great expectation for a coming Messiah who would return and establish heaven on earth.

Chapter Twenty-Two

ANGEL-YAHWEH

Many scholars believe that the angel of the LORD in the Old Testament is Jesus pre-incarnate.[18] The Bible presents this angel as One who can speak for Yahweh and as Yahweh yet seemingly not be Yahweh. The narrative I want to lead you on is one where there are two powers in heaven– interacting in a mysterious yet beautiful dance throughout both testaments. Jesus is the Angel-Yahweh. Jesus was revealing Himself in the Old Testament as the angel of the LORD(Angel-Yahweh) as Jude declares:

Now I want to remind you, although you once fully knew it, that Jesus, who saved a people out of the land of Egypt, afterward destroyed those who did not believe. (Jude 5 ESV) Jude is making a profound statement by claiming Jesus led the people out of Egypt.[19] Yet when we read the book of Exodus, it is the angel of God or the angel of Yahweh who leads them out.

Then the angel of God who was going before the host of

---

[18] Incarnate means when a spirit or deity becomes embodied in human flesh. Pre-incarnate refers to Jesus prior to coming as a baby.

[19] The NIV translates Jude 5: "I want to remind you that the Lord at one time delivered his people out of Egypt." Bruce Metzger prefers the use of Jesus in Jude 5, stating that "Critical principles seem to require the adoption of *Ἰησοῦς"* pointing out that it was the best attested reading amongst the Greek witnesses."(Metzger Commentary on the NT, 724).

Israel moved and went behind them, and the pillar of cloud moved from before them and stood behind them.

(Exodus 14:19 ESV)

Yahweh seems to give this messenger or angel a special place in his story, i.e., history. Jesus is not just an angel, but he is the one sent to establish his role in the redemptive plan of all mankind, even before putting on human nature. And just as Jesus led Israel out of bondage as the angel of the LORD, he is leading us as well.

But now go, lead the people to the place about which I have spoken to you; behold, my angel shall go before you.

(Exodus 32:34 ESV).

The Angel of Yahweh was no ordinary angel. He was the one who was sent to deliver the people of our God, and He was to be obeyed. The Angel came to deliver the Israelites from bondage in Egypt.

The name Egypt is the *Mitzrayim* in the Hebrew text. The name comes from the Hebrew root word מצור (masor), which can mean to be caught between two narrow areas; to be in a double straight, almost like one is confined.

In the Name Translation Bible, Egypt is translated as double anxiety. *Mitzrayim* is a double plural proper noun that means double anxiety. I like to say that double anxiety is being anxious about your past and fearful about your future. You don't feel forgiven for your past sins, hence doubtful about your future, leaving you powerless in the present.

Historically, Egypt represented the bondage to sin and the devil. Yet the name Egypt means 'double anxiety,' which is the culture that produces sin. The idea that anxiety is plural is why Egypt means double anxiety. The environment of sin is usually a place of anxiety.

Moses wrote that Yahweh **"...sent an angel, and brought us out of Egypt(Double anxiety)"** (Numbers 20:16 TNT). *Malak* is usually translated as 'angel' in Hebrew but can also mean someone who is sent on a supernatural assignment or a messenger.

Jesus is one sent with a message and not some angel. The gospel of John refers to Jesus as the sent one. **"The work of God is this: to believe in the One he has sent"** (John 6:29 ESV). Though Jesus is veiled at times as the Angel of Yahweh in the Old Testament, He is fully unveiled as the Son of God in the New Testament. Even the Hebrew grammar teaches us that this Angel is uniquely connected to Yahweh.

WHEN WE CRIED TO YAHWEH(JEALOUS ONE), HE HEARD OUR VOICE, SENT AN ANGEL, AND BROUGHT US OUT OF EGYPT(DOUBLE ANXIETY). (NUMBERS 20:16 TNT)

Chapter Twenty-Three

COMPOUND WORDS

A compound is a word made up of two or more parts that work together as a unit to express a specific concept. When you combine the words "sun" and "day," you get Sunday, or combine the words "law" and "suit," you get "lawsuit." Asher Intrater, in his book, "Who Ate Lunch with Abraham," discussed the combination of the words angel and Yahweh to actually become a compound word or a "s'michut." Asher Intrater writes:

There is a grammatical form in both biblical and modern Hebrew called "s'michut." The word "s'michut" means to put two things close together so that they touch one another. This grammatical form is made up of two words put together. S'michut joins two nouns so that they define one another mutually and become one unit together.[20]

Asher describes the words "angel of the LORD" or "Malak-Yahweh" as a s'michut. *Malak* is the Hebrew word for "messenger or angel." By joining the words angel and Yahweh, we discover Jesus as Angel-Yahweh in the Old Testament. Though we use the term "Angel-Yahweh," we also could use "Messenger of Yahweh" or "Sent One With The Authority of Yahweh." The danger of using the word angel in relationship to

[20] Intrater, Asher . Who Ate Lunch with Abraham . Kindle Edition.

Jesus is to suggest he is a created being. Jesus is the eternal Son of God; he was sent with authority to the earth to save us.

Hebrews was written to quell the controversy of Jesus being a created being. The book of Hebrews begins with identifying Jesus as the Son of God and not merely as some angel. The book of Hebrews is based upon Psalm 110, the most quoted Psalm in the New Testament.

For to which of the angels did God ever say, "You are my Son, today I have begotten you?" Or again, "I will be to him a father, and he shall be to me a son" (Hebrews 1:5-6 NIV).

Only a son can make someone a father. Remember, if Jesus did not always exist, Yahweh could not have always been Father–and He never changes! The author of Hebrews is making a statement about who Jesus is.

He is the radiance of the glory of God and the exact imprint of his nature, and he upholds the universe by the word of his power. After making purification for sins, he sat down at the right hand of the Majesty on high, having become as much superior to angels as the name he has inherited is more excellent than theirs. (Hebrews 1:3-4 NIV)

Even though Jesus takes the role of the Angel-Yahweh in the Old Testament, Hebrews declares him to be the other power in heaven that sits at the right hand of the Father. He is superior to the angels!

And again, when he brings the firstborn into the world, he says, "Let all God's angels worship him." But of the Son he

says, "Your throne, O God, is forever and ever, the scepter of
uprightness is the scepter of your kingdom."

(Hebrews 1:6,8 NIV)

Here we see Yahweh declares, **"Your throne, O God,"** about
Jesus. Jesus has a God license! Just as Solomon ascended to the
throne of his father David, Jesus received all authority from His
Father's throne. Jesus was revealed in the Old Testament though
not by name. Jesus is the Angel-Yahweh of the Old Testament.
Asher Intrater writes:

*It was Angel-Yahweh who appeared to Moses at the burning bush. It
was Angel-Yahweh who split the Red Sea and brought the children of
Israel out from Egypt. It was also Angel-Yahweh who met with
Moses on Mount Sinai.*[21]

Even King David recognizes another figure who encamped
around him and delivered him. This figure was not Yahweh but
the One sent by him. **"The angel of the LORD encamps around
those who fear him, and delivers them"** (Psalm 34:7 ESV).

I believe there is solid evidence that Jesus is Angel-
Yahweh and that He is the other power of heaven. This figure in
the Old Testament foreshadows the second power of heaven not
yet revealed. Remember, Jesus taught who he was to his
disciples by pointing them to Moses and all the Prophets.

**"Did not the Messiah have to suffer these things and then
enter his glory?" He told them, "How foolish you are, and
how slow to believe all that the prophets have spoken! And**

---

[21] Intrater, Asher . Who Ate Lunch with Abraham . Kindle Edition.

beginning with Moses and all the Prophets, he explained to them what was said in all the Scriptures concerning himself (Luke 24:25-27 ESV).

Jesus spoke to the two disciples on the way to Emmaus about the importance of revealing who He was from the Hebraic Scriptures(i.e., the Old Testament.)

In the story of Peter Pan, we discover Peter has no shadow. It is bizarre for someone to lose their shadow and have to spend time recovering it. The author of Hebrews writes that **"the law has but a shadow of the good things to come instead of the true form of these realities"** (Hebrews 10:1 ESV). Many Christians today fail to embrace the Old Testament and discover these realities of things to come. When a light source shines on something or someone, a shadow appears. A darkened form of the object is seen, but its reality is not fully grasped. There are many Christians who are like Peter Pan who now must spend time recovering their shadow.

Every Christian ought to become a student of the entire Bible, fully pursuing and never forgetting the need to be grounded in the rich soil of Moses and the Prophets. Christians must never lose focus concerning the centrality of Jesus in our lives and the Biblical narrative. What a day it will be when every believer sees Jesus stepping out of the shadow of the Old Testament and into the fullness of light in the New Testament!

Chapter Twenty-Four

MY FATHER'S NAME

Jesus also declares that he walks in the authority of his Father's name. **"I have come in my Father's name, and you do not accept me"** (John 5:43 ESV). Jesus claims his abilities are to testify about the name of his Father. **"The works I do in my Father's name testify about me"** (John 10:25 ESV). Some of the last words of Jesus are a prayer concerning the power of his name:

> **Holy Father, protect them by the power of your name, the name you gave me, so that they may be one as we are one. While I was with them, I protected them and kept them safe by that name you gave me.** (John 17:11-12 ESV)

Yahweh tells the Israelites that Angel-Yahweh has His name in Him.

> **See, I am sending an angel ahead of you to guard you along the way and to bring you to the place I have prepared. Pay attention to him and listen to what he says. Do not rebel against him; he will not forgive your rebellion, since my Name is in him.** (Exodus 23:20-21 NIV)

Here is the job description of Angel-Yahweh:

1) **Sent to the Israelites**
2) **Guarded them on the way**
3) **Brought them into a prepared place**
4) **Must be paid attention to**

5) Not to be rebelled against

6) Unwilling to forgive rebellion

This angel is so powerful that the Israelites are warned not to rebel against him. If they do rebel, this angel or messenger will not forgive them.

Like Angel-Yahweh, Jesus was questioned about his authority to forgive sins, and the Jews recognized the authority of this statement.

And when Jesus saw their faith, he said to the paralytic, "Son, your sins are forgiven." Now some of the scribes were sitting there, questioning in their hearts, "Why does this man speak like that? He is blaspheming! Who can forgive sins but God alone?" (Mark 2:5-7 ESV)

The scribes failed to realize that Yahweh was not the only one with authority to forgive sins. There were two powers who had the power to forgive sins.

But that you may know that the Son of Man has authority on earth to forgive sins"—he said to the paralytic— "I say to you, rise, pick up your bed, and go home." (Mark 2:10 ESV)

Often when Angel-Yahweh is speaking, he will speak as Yahweh himself. When I see this, I am reminded of the Jewish ceremony called the "Bar-Mitzvah." Every Jewish boy will experience this ceremony where he transitions from a child to a man. After his father blesses him, saying, "You are my son, whom I love. In you I delight," the son from this point forward may do business in the marketplace in his father's name.

Jesus received his father's blessing at the Jordan, and the voice from heaven spoke these same words. From this point forward, the ministry of Jesus exploded in the supernatural business of heaven.

If you listen carefully to what he says and do all that I say, I will be an enemy to your enemies and will oppose those who oppose you. My angel will go ahead of you and bring you into the land… and I will wipe them out. (Exodus 23:22-23) Jesus is the Angel of Yahweh who brings His people into the Promised Land. We come into the land when we follow the Lamb. The Angel of the LORD is seen as partnering with man and Yahweh to bring redemption.

THE FATHER-SON CONNECTION HAS BEEN LOST IN MANY CULTURES, BUT AS WE LOOK TO THE JEWS, WE FIND THEY HAVE CREATED A CEREMONY THAT HAS BEEN PASSED ON FROM GENERATION TO GENERATION TO PRESERVE THIS CONNECTION. THIS CEREMONY IS CALLED A "BAR MITZVAH. "THE "BAR MITZVAH" IS A PART OF JEWISH CULTURE THAT I WISH ALL CHRISTIANS PARTICIPATED IN. THE WORD "BAR MITZVAH" MEANS "SON OF THE LAW" AND INSTILLS A POWERFUL MESSAGE TO THE NEXT GENERATION, FROM FATHER TO SON.

Chapter Twenty-Five

WHO IS WHO?

Interestingly, the first time the Angel-Yahweh appears in the Bible is to speak to Hagar, an Egyptian slave. She had just run away from her jealous, harsh master's wife, who was angry over her pregnancy.

Angel-Yahweh(*The Messenger of the Jealous one*) said to her, "Behold, you are with child, and will bear a son. You will call his name Ishmael(*God listens*) because Yahweh(*Jealous one*) has heard your affliction." She called on the name of Yahweh(*Jealous one*), who spoke to her, "You are a God who sees," for she said, "Have I even stayed alive after seeing him?" (Genesis 16:11,13 TNT)

We discover that the Hagar then calls on the name of Yahweh, who spoke to her. But didn't she speak to Angel-Yahweh? We find this strange phenomenon happening over and over again, where Yahweh and Angel-Yahweh are inseparable.

Angel-Yahweh(*Jealous one*) called to Abraham(*Father of nations*) a second time out of the sky, and said, "I have sworn by myself," says Yahweh(*Jealous one*), "because you have done this thing, and have not withheld your son, your only son, that I will bless you greatly" (Genesis 21:15-17 TNT)

Here again, Angel-Yahweh calls to Abraham and speaks as Yahweh. Angel-Yahweh can do the business of heaven on earth and carries the authority of the name of Yahweh. But we should not make the mistake of claiming they are the same person.

As the Israelites enter the Promised Land and fail to drive out all the Canaanites, the Angel-Yahweh once again appears:

Angel-Yahweh(*Messenger of the Jealous one*) came up from Gilgal(*Roll away*) to Bochim(*Crying people*). He said, "I brought you out of Egypt(*Double anxiety*) and have brought you to the land which I swore to give your fathers. I said, 'I will never break my covenant with you. You will make no covenant with the inhabitants of this land. You will break down their altars.' But you have not listened to my voice. Why have you done this? Therefore, I also said, 'I will not drive them out from before you; but they will be in your sides, and their gods will be a snare to you.'" When Angel-Yahweh(*Messenger of the Jealous one*) spoke these words to all the children of Israel(*Struggler with God*), the people lifted up their voice, and wept. (Judges 2:1-4 TNT)

Here are the claims of Angel-Yahweh from this verse:

1. I brought you out of Egypt

2. I made a covenant with you that can be broken

3. I brought you into the Promised Land

4. The people of Israel failed to listen to Him

5. Bondage will result from not heeding the voice of Angel-Yahweh

These are powerful claims that only someone very unique could declare.

75

When Jacob was blessing his son Joseph, he mentioned the God of Abraham and Isaac and the angel who redeemed him from all evil. Interestingly, Jacob honors two powers in heaven as he passes on his generational blessing.

He blessed Joseph(*May He add*), and said, "The God before whom my fathers' Abraham(*Father of nations*) and Isaac(*Laughter*) walked, the God who has fed me all my life long to this day, the Angel who has redeemed me from all evil, bless the boys, and let my name be named on them, and the name of my fathers" (Genesis 48:15-16 TNT)

The blessing of Jacob's descendants noted this angel because this was no ordinary angel. The patriarchs of the Old Testament readily acknowledged this second power of heaven as separate from Yahweh.

JEWISH CULTURE DECLARES THAT THE NAMES OF THE FATHER WERE INCLUDED AS PART OF THE NAME OF THE SON. JESUS REPLIED, "BLESSED ARE YOU, SIMON SON OF JONAH, FOR THIS WAS NOT REVEALED TO YOU BY FLESH AND BLOOD, BUT BY MY FATHER IN HEAVEN." (MATTHEW 16:17) THE SON AND FATHER WERE SO CONNECTED IN ANCIENT TIMES THAT SIMON (OR PETER) WAS KNOWN AS "SIMON SON OF JONAH."

Chapter Twenty-Six

SEE HIM AND DIE

As you look closely at the Scriptures, we see a pattern of Angel-Yahweh making claims for which Yahweh would naturally be credited. Gideon also had an encounter with Angel-Yahweh.

Then Angel-Yahweh(*Messenger of the Jealous one*) departed out of his sight. Gideon(*Hacker*) saw that he was Angel-Yahweh(*Messenger of the Jealous one*) and Gideon(Hacker) said, "Alas, Lord Yahweh(*Jealous one*)! Because I have seen Angel-Yahweh(*Messenger of the Jealous one*) face to face!" Yahweh(*Jealous one*) said to him, "Peace be to you! Do not be afraid. You will not die." (Judges 6:21-23 TNT)

Who is this angel that Gideon cried out to Yahweh in fear of dying after seeing Him? Gideon believed if anyone saw the face of our God, they would die. Years earlier, Yahweh told Moses, **"You cannot see my face, for man may not see me and live"** (Exodus 33:20 ESV). Gideon's statement is significant because he sees Angel-Yahweh with the same kind of authority and then expects death to ensue. The parents of Samson felt the same awe in the presence of Angel-Yahweh.

Then Manoah(*Rest*) knew that he was Angel-Yahweh (*Messenger of the Jealous one*). Manoah(*Rest*) said to his wife, "We will surely die because we have seen our God."

(Judges 13:22 TNT)

77

To Manoah, seeing Angel-Yahweh and seeing Yahweh had the same result– death! The person of Angel-Yahweh and Yahweh seems indistinguishable at times!

Leviticus chapter 10 describes an event where the sons of Aaron saw Yahweh and died. Two of Aaron's sons failed to burn the right incense and used a fire that was not authorized. Yahweh commanded the burning of a certain incense that released a thick smoke that would completely cover the Ark of the Covenant. The smoke that was released from the authorized incense covered the LORD so that He could remain unseen. I believe Nadab and Abihu died because the smoke released from their unauthorized incense failed to cover the appearance of Yahweh. They saw Him and died on the spot.

Aaron's sons Nadab and Abihu took their censers, put fire in them, and added incense; and they offered unauthorized fire before the LORD, contrary to his command. So, fire came out from the presence of the LORD and consumed them, and they died before the LORD. (Leviticus 10:1-2 NIV)

The parents of Samson were legitimately afraid because they saw the appearance of their God in the Angel-Yahweh. They asked for His name because they knew that His name was not Yahweh. Angel-Yahweh replied, **"Why do you ask about my name since it is wonderful?"** (Judges 13:18 TNT). The Hebrew word 'wonderful' is pali and means "wonderful, beyond understanding."[22]

---

[22] Strong's Concordance

Though Samson's parents ask for His name, He does not give it to them yet tells them it is beyond understanding. Some translate Isaiah 9:6, confirming that the Son is the Wonderful(*pali*) Counselor.

For to us a child is born, to us a son is given; and the government shall be upon his shoulder, and his name shall be called Wonderful Counselor, Mighty God, Everlasting Father, Prince of Peace. (Isaiah 9:6 ESV)

MANY BIBLE TEACHERS TEACH THAT GOD HAS MANY NAMES, BUT IN FACT HE HAS ONLY ONE NAME. THE FOUR LETTERS THAT MAKE UP THIS NAME, YHWH, ARE CALLED THE TETRAGRAMMATON. JEWS FOR CENTURIES HAVE REFRAINED FROM EVER SAYING THE HOLY NAME OF GOD IN FEAR OF BEING IRREVERENT. 'YAHWEH' IS THE MOST COMMON WAY TO PRONOUNCE THE TETRAGRAMMATON, YET OTHERS HAVE USED THE PRONUNCIATION 'JEHOVAH.' SINCE HEBREW WAS A SPOKEN LANGUAGE MORE THAN A WRITTEN LANGUAGE, VOWELS WERE NOT PLACED IN THE TEXTS UNTIL ABOUT THE SIXTH CENTURY A.D. WITH ONLY THE CONSONANTS PLACED IN THE HEBREW TEXT, WE ARE LEFT WITH ONLY A GUESS OF HOW TO PRONOUNCE HIS NAME.

Chapter Twenty-Seven

PROPHECY FULFILLED

The word "angel" can mean a messenger or someone in service to bring a message. The book of Zechariah has a tremendous amount of dialogue from Angel-Yahweh that is highlighted in The Name Translation Bible in purple. Jesus speaks in the Old Testament in the book of Zechariah:

I said to them, "If you think it best, give me my wages; and if not, keep them." So, they weighed for my wages thirty pieces of silver. (Zechariah 11:12 TNT)

The book of Zechariah declares the price by which Judas Iscariot would sell Jesus off to His enemies.

Then one of the twelve, whose name was Judas Iscariot, went to the chief priests and said, "What will you give me if I deliver him over to you?" And they paid him thirty pieces of silver. And from that moment he sought an opportunity to betray him. (Matthew 26:14-16 ESV)

Jesus invited Judas onto his team, knowing he would betray Him one day. Judas loved money and bargained for the highest price he could receive for his betrayal. Every time we gather to take Communion, Paul reminds us to remember it happened in the context of betrayal.

For I received from the Lord that which also I delivered to you, that the Lord Jesus on the night in which he was betrayed took bread (1 Corinthians 11:23 WEB).

Just as it was spoken by Angel-Yahweh in the book of Zechariah, Judas agrees to betray Jesus for thirty pieces of silver and brings his enemies to the place where Jesus was praying. The chief priests paid for the betrayal of Jesus through the temple's firstborn son fund. Every firstborn of Israel belonged to the LORD and had to be purchased back from the temple.

So, Moses took the redemption money from those who were over and above those redeemed by the Levites. From the firstborn of the people of Israel he took the money.

(Numbers 3:49-50 ESV)

The same money obtained for redemption led to the betrayal of Jesus, which in turn led to our redemption. The gospel of Matthew reveals the prophetic fulfillment.

Then was fulfilled what had been spoken by the prophet Jeremiah, saying, "And they took the thirty pieces of silver, the price of him on whom a price had been set by some of the sons of Israel, and they gave them for the potter's field, as the Lord directed me" (Matthew 27:3-10 ESV.)

Matthew assigns this prophecy to Jeremiah even though most of it is in the book of Zechariah. Matthew is likely referring to the Jeremiah scroll, which also contains the book of Zechariah.[23]

---

[23]The less likely possibility is Matthew is referring the field that Jeremiah bought in chapter 32 or the pottery he purchased in chapter 19.

In Zechariah 11:12, Angel-Yahweh is saying I worked as a shepherd, now pay me my wages! He went to those he worked for and asked them to pay him what they thought he was worth. They gave him thirty pieces of silver– not the earnings of a shepherd, but the price paid for an enslaved person's accidental death. **"If the ox gores a slave, male or female, the owner shall give to their master thirty shekels of silver"** (Exodus 21:32 ESV). The Jewish religious establishment rejected Jesus as their shepherd and treated him like a slave whose death was an accident. Yahweh commands Angel-Yahweh to give back their insulting excuse for a wage and throw it into the temple.

Yahweh(*Jealous one*) said to me, "Throw it to the potter, the handsome price that I was valued at by them!" I took the thirty pieces of silver, and threw them to the potter, in the house of Yahweh(*Jealous one*). (Zechariah 11:13 TNT) Jesus' death was not accidental but orchestrated before time began–not spilled blood but intentional. Everything we read in the Scriptures points to its fulfillment in Christ Jesus.

Then when Judas, his betrayer, saw that Jesus was condemned, he changed his mind and brought back the thirty pieces of silver to the chief priests and the elders, saying: "I have sinned by betraying innocent blood." They said, "What is that to us? See to it yourself." And throwing down the pieces of silver into the temple, he departed, and he went and hanged himself. (Matthew 27:6-8 ESV) Judas feels remorse and throws the money into the temple, fulfilling the prophetic word. But because it is blood money, the priests decide to buy a field with it instead of putting it back in the treasury.

But the chief priests, taking the pieces of silver, said, "It is not lawful to put them into the treasury, since it is blood money." So, they took counsel and bought with them the potter's field as a burial place for strangers. Therefore, that field has been called the Field of Blood to this day.
(Matthew 27:3-10 ESV)

Fulfilling the words of Angel-Yahweh in the book of Zechariah, the payment of thirty shekels released Jesus from serving in the temple. But before Jesus' crucifixion, Judas returned the money, obligating Jesus to serve in the temple. Jesus could not be the high priest if he was dismissed from serving in the temple!

What did the chief priests do with the money? They used it to buy a field as a burial place for foreigners. The money used to betray Jesus secured a place for Gentiles after they had died. Zechariah 11:13 says, **"Throw it to the potter."** What would a potter be doing in the temple during the times of Zechariah, and why would you throw thirty shekels at him? The book of Zechariah paints a prophetic picture of the money going through the hands of the priests and landing in the potter's hands to purchase the field. Was this also the prophetic fulfillment of Isaiah 53:12? Yahweh declares of His servant in this verse:

Because he poured out his soul to death and was numbered with the transgressors; yet he bore the sin of many, and makes intercession for the transgressors. (Isaiah 53:12 ESV)

Jesus' betrayal allowed us to share in His grace after we die. He bore the sin of many and numbered Himself with us so that we could share in His glory.

IMAGINE THE IMPACT OF MAKING COVENANT WITH ANOTHER PARTY. ONCE THE COVENANT WAS CUT, BOTH PARTIES WOULD WALK IN GREATER CONFIDENCE THROUGHOUT LIFE, KNOWING THEY WERE NOT ALONE. BEING IN COVENANT MEANS BEING "ONE" IN HEART WITH EACH ANOTHER. TO THE ANCIENTS, EVERY ACT WAS VIEWED AS RIGHTEOUS OR UNRIGHTEOUS, ACCORDING TO ONE'S LOYALTY TO THE COVENANT. SADLY TODAY, MOST OF US HAVE LOST THE DEEP UNDERSTANDING OF COVENANT. WE HAVE NO CLUE THAT WE ARE LIVING SUCH EMPTY LIVES BECAUSE WE LACK COVENANT RELATIONSHIPS. ONE INTERESTING DYNAMIC IN THE HEBREW LANGUAGE WAS THAT THE WORD "FRIEND" ONLY APPLIED TO THOSE WITH WHO YOU WERE IN COVENANT. "GREATER LOVE HAS NO ONE THAN THIS, THAT HE LAY DOWN HIS LIFE FOR HIS FRIENDS" (JOHN 15:13).

Chapter Twenty-Eight

CHRISTOPHANY

John writes in his gospel about the prophet Isaiah seeing the glory of Jesus. **"Isaiah said this because he saw Jesus' glory and spoke about him"** (John 12:41 NIV). How did Isaiah see the glory of Jesus seven hundred years before He was even born? Was Isaiah referring to the Suffering Servant passages in chapter 53? Or is John describing the event in Isaiah 6 after King Uzziah died: **"I saw the Lord sitting upon a throne, high and lifted up; and the train of his robe filled the temple"** (Isaiah 6:1 NIV)?

When we see the word 'Lord' in most translations, it refers to a title given to someone. 'Lord' (*Adonai* in Hebrew) is the title Jesus was assigned most often in the New Testament. "Jesus is Lord" is the confession that saves us according to Romans 10:9. Paul writes: **"If you confess with your mouth that Jesus is Lord... you will be saved."** Though Yahweh is also referred to as Lord(*Adonai*) in the Old Testament, the use of the word may point us to the Christ. Many verses in the Old Testament are positioned to be fully unveiled in the New Testament.

Did Isaiah see the glory of Jesus at this moment when he said, "I saw Adonai?" A few verses later, we read, **"Behold, this has touched your lips; your guilt is taken away, and your sin**

atoned for" (Isaiah 6:7). Only after we have had our guilt taken away can we boldly ask to be sent out into our world. Isaiah then responds, **"Here I am. Send me"** (Isaiah 6:8).

Isaiah sees and writes about the crucifixion of Christ seven hundred years before it even happens. He confidently declares our healing and forgiveness as being a completed event even prior to it happening.

Surely, he has borne our griefs and carried our sorrows; yet we esteemed him stricken, smitten by our God, and afflicted. But he was pierced for our transgressions; he was crushed for our iniquities; upon him was the chastisement that brought us peace, and with his wounds we are healed.

(Isaiah 53:4-5 ESV)

Experiencing the glory of Jesus will release us into our calling. Jesus Christ, the Son of God, must become preeminent in our lives! Preeminent means to be superior to or notable above all others. Our gospel must be centered on the person of Jesus.

We must also see the glory of Jesus in the Old Testament just like Isaiah saw his glory. Jesus' appearance in the Old Testament is like a scene in a movie where a character is revealed and made significant, yet this character never fulfills his role in the plot. Directors will often introduce a character into a movie in this manner if they are planning a sequel. Those who watch the movie understand that a sequel is coming soon so that this significant character's role will be fulfilled.

When Jesus appears in the Old Testament, this phenomenon is called a "Christophany." A Christophany notifies the reader that an undisclosed figure(who is the Christ) will soon be revealed, which is the Greek word *"phany."*

In the Name Translation Bible, I highlight the differences between the words of the Father(Yahweh), the words of the Son(Jesus), and the words of the pre-incarnate Jesus. To help the readers identify who is speaking, I used the following color code when applicable in my translation:

a. Red is the color of the earth(i.e., red clay) and represents the words of Jesus, the Son

b. Blue is the color of the heavens(or the sky) and represents the words of Yahweh, the Father

c. Purple is the color of royalty and represents the words of the pre-incarnate Christ(Angel-Yahweh, Melchizedek, I AM, etc.)

Many translations highlight the words of Jesus in red, yet when Yahweh, the Father, speaks, his words remain undistinguished. Adding the color purple to the translation helps readers see when Jesus is speaking in the Old Testament. When the reader sees the words in purple, it allows the reader to better recognize a likely Christophany.

Jesus is the character in the Old Testament that is fully revealed and fulfilled in the New Testament. The two powers of heaven work together to redeem mankind and to model a Father-Son relationship. I will discuss a few times that Jesus steps onto the scene in the Old Testament.

Chapter Twenty-Nine

WHO IS "I AM"

My understanding of the I AM has changed in the last decade. One author said that most of his current books were written to correct the errors of his previous books! In pursuit of the truth, every theologian must be willing to change their views as we are confronted by a new understanding or a missing piece in the puzzle. Just like the apostle Paul changed his theology after he was knocked off his horse, all of those who study the Bible must recognize our own limitations.

I previously understood that Yahweh was the "I AM." I had written that Jesus was not claiming to be the "I AM." My concern was confusing who the Father is and who Jesus is. I changed my view that Jesus was claiming to be the "I AM." **"Very truly I tell you," Jesus answered, "before Abraham was born, I AM!"** (John 8:58 NIV)). Jesus declares he was the "I AM" of the Old Testament. The "I AM" is not Yahweh but Jesus.

Some scholars understand the name Yahweh to mean "You are" or "You exist!" We could say, "Yahweh is the 'You Are!' and Jesus is the 'I AM!'" *Ego eimi* is the Greek phrase that means "I AM."

Your father Abraham rejoiced at the thought of seeing my day; he saw it and was glad." "You are not yet fifty years old," they said to him, "and you have seen Abraham!" "Very

truly I tell you," Jesus answered, "before Abraham was born, I am!" (John 8:56-58 NIV)

Jesus only left them three options: He was insane, He was a blasphemer, or to believe that He was the Son of Man. Asher Intrater wrote, *"For the religious leaders of the first century, deciding between Jesus' insanity or His divinity was not a very easy choice."*[24]

Jesus was criticized by Jewish leadership because they assumed he spoke of the destruction of their temple. Jesus knew that He would become the center of worship for all people, and His body would become the new temple.

Jesus answered them, "Destroy this temple, and in three days, I will raise it up." The Jews then said, "It has taken forty-six years to build this temple, and will you raise it up in three days?" (John 2:19-20 ESV)

Interestingly, the Jews did not understand He was speaking of His own body as the temple. Our DNA is the blueprint of our body, and our DNA consists of forty-six strands. The Jews mention forty-six years in regard to the age of the temple but prophetically speak to the number of strands of the very DNA of the future temple. The resurrection of Jesus has established the new temple on earth– His body. Jesus, the Son of God, takes center stage. This became controversial to the Jews in the 1st century and beyond.

[24] Intrater, Asher . Who Ate Lunch with Abraham . Kindle Edition.

The Old Testament does prepare the Jew for the coming of Jesus. When Jesus said, **"Before Abraham was born, I AM,"** He was pointing them to His role as the other power in heaven.

The first mention of the I AM in the Bible is found in the story of Moses prior to being sent by the LORD to free the Israelites from slavery in Egypt. When Moses sees the burning bush, notice both Yahweh and the Angel-Yahweh are in the fire. **Angel-Yahweh(*Messenger of the Jealous one*) appeared to him in a flame of fire out of the middle of a bush. He looked, and behold, the bush burned with fire, and the bush was not consumed. Moses said, "I will turn aside now, and see this great sight, why the bush is not burned." When Yahweh(*Jealous one*) saw that he turned aside to see.** (Exodus 3:2-4 TNT)

In my previous book, Heaven's Dynasty, I go into detail about the phrase *ego eimi* and show how it is commonly used to say, "I AM." Since writing the book, I have discovered that both Jesus and Yahweh may have been in the bush, and both spoke to Moses.

One day, Moses was caring for sheep on the other side of the desert when he came upon a burning bush. The angel of the LORD then appeared to him in the flames of fire. When Moses heard a voice from the bush, he was hearing both the voice of Yahweh and the voice of Jesus.

Moses said to God, "Suppose I go to the Israelites and say to them, 'The God of your fathers has sent me to you,' and they

ask me, 'What is his name?' Then what shall I tell them?"

(Exodus 3:13 NIV)

So, Moses is talking to a burning bush, hoping to get a name.

And God said to Moses, "I AM who I AM. This is what you are to say to the Israelites: 'I AM has sent me to you.'"

(Exodus 3:13 NIV)

I can imagine Moses writing the name down and making a mental note. But then in the next verse, we read:

God also said to Moses, "Say to the Israelites, 'Yahweh, the God of your fathers-the God of Abraham, the God of Isaac and the God of Jacob-has sent me to you.' "This is my name forever, the name you shall call me from generation to generation. (Exodus 3:15-16 NIV).

Moses then crosses out "I AM" and writes Yahweh? Wait, who is sending me? Is it Yahweh or is it I AM? What if there were both Jesus and Yahweh in the bush? What if both powers of heaven were in the bush? Since Angel-Yahweh took a prominent role in delivering the Jews out of Egypt, it would make sense for Him to be present in the bush.

IN SPACE TRAVEL, YOUR TRAJECTORY WILL DETERMINE YOUR DESTINATION. A SMALL SHIFT IN TRAJECTORY WILL PUT YOU IN A COMPLETELY DIFFERENT LOCATION.

Chapter Thirty

JESUS IS LORD

We read in Psalm 2 where Yahweh and his Anointed are being plotted against by the kings of the earth.

The kings of the earth take a stand and the rulers take counsel together against Yahweh, and against his Anointed.

(Psalm 2:2 WEB)

Yahweh and his Anointed are the Father and Son who co-rule together on one throne. The Bible also declares that there is only one throne on which the Father and Son sit, and upon this throne, the kingdom of God will be established upon the earth. Interestingly, Psalm 2 ends with the command to **"Kiss the Son"** (vs.12) so that you will not incur the wrath of Yahweh.

Now that Jesus is ruling, there is a clear focus we must place on the name of Jesus. Because the Son is seated at the right hand of the Father and **"All authority in Heaven and Earth has been given to him..."** (Matthew 28:20), we must lead people to Him, so they can have access to the Father. In John 14:6, Jesus said, **"I am the way and the truth and the life. No one comes to the Father except through me"** (John 14:6).

The Westernized Christian message is "Jesus is God." Yet, the early church never preached this message. Their message was "Jesus is the Son of God" as we read in Acts: **"At once, he began to preach in the synagogues that Jesus is the Son of**

God" (Acts 9:20 NIV). What is the difference, you might ask? The difference is subtle but very important. By declaring that Jesus is God, we are actually saying that Jesus is the Father, or Jesus is Yahweh. As I read the Bible, I find the idea of Jesus being called 'God'(though he has a God-license) being forced into the text of the Bible. Embracing Jesus as the second power of heaven– someone who is not Yahweh but instead Yahweh's Son.

Jesus assumes the title of Lord so as to distinguish himself from Yahweh. Jesus was given all authority in heaven and on earth by the Father. He will rule until he places all things that come under His rule. Then He will submit himself back to the Father.

For he must reign until he has put all his enemies under his feet. The last enemy to be destroyed is death. For he "has put everything under his feet." Now when it says that "everything" has been put under him, it is clear that this does not include God himself, who put everything under Christ. When he has done this, then the Son himself will be made subject to him who put everything under him, so that God may be all in all. (1 Corinthians 15:25-28 NIV)

Note that Paul redefines "everything" so as to exclude God Himself from everything placed under the feet of Jesus. The ultimate goal is to put everything under His feet or everything in line with God's rule. The kingdom of God is wherever God's rule is obeyed without question or hesitation.

Jesus is like gravity. He is an invisible force that surrounds us, who we must recognize continually and live governed by Him. When we fail to recognize this force, we fall, we break stuff, and we hurt ourselves and others. Gravity keeps us down to earth, and in Him, we live and move and have our being. We may not thank God daily for gravity, but without it, the universe would fall apart. Gravity governs the universe. Without it, we would all be torn apart. Gravity provides a relationship between all that is in the universe. Jesus is the governing force that we all must submit. Yes, many ignore Him, avoid Him, and exclude Him but the fact remains: pain will ensue when this governing force is denied.

Jesus said, **"You will know the truth, and the truth will set you free."** Truth can be defined as *"an actual event or state, reality."*[25] When we live fully understanding reality, we have freedom. Gravity to the natural realm is what Jesus is to the spiritual realm. Paul writes these powerful words about Jesus to the church of Colossians:

He is the image of the invisible God, the firstborn of all creation. For by him all things were created, in heaven and on earth, visible and invisible, whether thrones or dominions or rulers or authorities—all things were created through him and for him. And he is before all things, and in him all things hold together. And he is the head of the body, the church. He is the beginning, the firstborn from the dead, that in everything he might be preeminent. For in him all the fullness of God was pleased to dwell, and through him to

---

[25] Accordance definition ἀλήθειαν in English Lexicon of the New Testament:

reconcile to himself all things, whether on earth or in heaven, making peace by the blood of his cross.

(Colossians 1:15-20 ESV)

Paul writes these powerful words about Jesus and declares his preeminence above all. Everything our God was, Jesus was– not in some mysterious manner as often communicated through theology, but in a simple, beautiful way. Like a Father releasing His Son into His royal position. Paul defines what we have through Jesus before God. Jesus Christ is God's Son who opens the way for us before God the Father. **"Such is the confidence we have through the Anointed One toward our God"** (2 Corinthians 3:4 TNT).

JOHN ADAMS WAS THE SECOND PRESIDENT OF THE UNITED STATES AND HIS SON, JOHN QUINCY, SERVED AS PRESIDENT FOUR TERMS LATER. WE SHOULD HONOR THE POSITION TO WHICH THE SON HAS ASCENDED AND TREAT HIM NO DIFFERENTLY THAN WE WOULD TREAT HIS FATHER. JESUS ASSUMES THE "GOD" POSITION LIKE HIS FATHER, THOUGH WE SHOULD REFER TO HIM AS 'LORD' TO SIGNIFY THE DIFFERENCE. WE DO NOT HAVE TO MAKE JESUS PART OF YAHWEH IN SOME MYSTERIOUS ONENESS TO BE BIBLICAL.

Chapter Thirty-One

THE MESSIAH

Jesus is the "Anointed One" or the one marked with oil to signify his authority to sit on the royal throne. The Anointed One is spoken of throughout the Old Testament. Both the word "Messiah" in Hebrew and "Christ" in Greek mean one anointed with oil. **"For the one whom God has sent speaks the words of God, for God gives the Spirit without limit"** (John 3:34 NIV). The Jewish people were expecting a Messiah to come, and one of the characteristics of this Messiah would be that He would be able to release the Spirit without limit. Throughout the Bible, one leader would transfer his mantle or his spirit onto one person to be his replacement. Moses passed on his leadership to Joshua, Elijah to Elisha, and David to Solomon, to name a few.

What set apart the Messiah was that he would have an unending Spirit to transfer authority and power to whoever wanted His mantle. Jesus was not limited to one person to whom he could pass on his mantle. When Jesus ascended to the throne of heaven, kingdom authority was released on earth. His disciples who were waiting for this baptism experience the Spirit transference.

The Holy Spirit is the mantle transference. Elijah and Elisha walked together. One was taken away, and the other received a mantle that belonged to the other. Jesus offers you and I and the Holy Spirit so that we can do everything He did! But this mantle is only transferred as we walk with Jesus and see Him for who He really is!

The Jordan is the place where mantles are transferred. Jordan in Hebrew refers to a place of descent. A mantle is the advancement of another generation passed on to empower the next generation. The mantle must be honored and humbly received to receive its benefits. John the Baptist, a descendant of a high priest, immersed Jesus, passing the mantle of the high priest to Jesus. The Old Testament also describes another mantle transference that took place at the Jordan. When Elijah was taken up to heaven, he left behind his cloak for Elisha to take upon himself. The cloak represents the mantle of ministry Elijah was passing on to Elisha.

And he took up the cloak of Elijah that had fallen from him and went back and stood on the bank of the Jordan.

(2 Kings 2:13 ESV)

The word for cloak in Hebrew is *adderet*. It is derived from the root word *adar*, which means *"to make majestic or powerful."*[26] The mantle is placed upon us, and we need to grow into it. Just like bigger clothes are bought for children as they are growing, the LORD provides us mantles that are bigger than we are so that we might grow into them. Elijah passed his mantle on before he went to heaven, but Elisha's mantle was left in his tomb when he died. We can assume this to be true, not only because greedy

---

[26] Strong's Concordance

Gehazi failed to be his successor, but because a dead man came back to life after touching the bones of Elisha.

And as a man was being buried, behold, a marauding band was seen, and the man was thrown into the grave of Elisha, and as soon as the man touched the bones of Elisha, he revived and stood on his feet. (2 Kings 13:21 ESV)

This portion of Scripture reminds us that mantles will lay dormant in cemeteries if they are not passed on to the next generation. Recover every mantle from the past so that we lack nothing in the present.

THE SPIRIT COMES ON US WHEN WE BEGIN WALKING IN OUR ANOINTED IDENTITY. JESUS BEGAN HIS MINISTRY ONCE HE RECEIVED HIS FATHER'S BLESSING. WHEN HE HEARD HIS FATHER'S WORDS— THIS WAS THE ANOINTING THAT MARKED HIM AS A CANDIDATE FOR THE SPIRIT OF SONSHIP. ISAIAH 61:1 SAYS, "THE SPIRIT OF THE SOVEREIGN LORD IS ON ME, BECAUSE THE LORD HAS ANOINTED ME." CHRIST'S FOLLOWERS ARE CALLED CHRISTIANS OR "ANOINTED ONES OR SMEARED ONES." CHRISTIANS ARE MARKED BY HEAVEN AS SONS AND DAUGHTERS, DESTINED FOR GREATNESS AND EMPOWERED BY THE FATHER'S BLESSING.

Chapter Thirty-Two

SERVANT OF YAHWEH

The Servant of Yahweh reveals Jesus in the Old Testament. In the TNT version, the words in verses 1-3a are in purple to signify the appearance of Jesus in the Old Testament:

Listen, islands, to me. Listen, you peoples, from afar: Yahweh(*Jealous one*) has called me from the womb; from the inside of my mother, he has mentioned my name. He has made my mouth like a sharp sword. He has hidden me in the shadow of his hand. He has made me a polished shaft. He has kept me close in his quiver. He said to me, "You are my servant; Israel(*Struggler with God*), in whom I will be glorified." (Isaiah 49:1-3 TNT)

The Servant is called "Israel" in this passage, which can also mean "Prince of our God." Some rabbis claim that the Suffering Servant in these passages is the nation of Israel. Yet as we continue reading. We discover that this Servant is reaching out to gather Israel back to Yahweh.

Now Yahweh, he who formed me from the womb to be his Servant, says to bring Jacob(*Heel grabber*) again to him, and to gather Israel(*Struggler with God*) to him, for I am honorable in the eyes of Yahweh(*Jealous one*), and my God has become my strength. (Isaiah 49:5 TNT)

Distinguishing the voice of the Servant of Yahweh from the voice of Yahweh and the voice of Isaiah helps us see prophetic elements in these verses.

I gave my back to those who beat me, and my cheeks to those who plucked off the hair. I did not hide my face from shame and spitting. For the Lord Yahweh(*Jealous one*) will help me. Therefore, I have not been confounded. Therefore, I have set my face like a flint, and I know that I will not be disappointed. (Isaiah 50:6-7 TNT)

The New Testament never records Jesus' beard being ripped off his face, but Isaiah saw it seven hundred years before it happened! The gospel of Matthew profoundly describes the Suffering Servant of Isaiah: **"Then they spit in his face and struck him. And some slapped him"**(Matthew 26:67 ESV). Jesus is the Servant in the Book of Isaiah.

One of the most significant misinterpretations by Jews is to claim that the nation of Israel is the Servant of Isaiah 53. Yet throughout Jewish history, rabbis saw this passage as referring to the Messiah. I believe modern rabbis have sought to sway people to this point of view because Jesus fulfills these ancient words so wholly. Isaiah 53 paints an undeniable picture of the entire crucifixion– a practice not yet invented in Isaiah's time– yet written as if he was at the very foot of the cross.

He was despised, and rejected by men; a man of suffering, and acquainted with disease. He was despised as one from whom men hide their face; and we did not respect him. Surely, he has borne our sickness, and carried our suffering;

yet we considered him plagued, struck by our God, and afflicted. But he was pierced for our transgressions. He was crushed for our iniquities. The punishment that brought our peace was on him; and by his wounds we are healed. (Isaiah 53:3-5 TNT)

To deny the Messiah this prophetic statement and claim it for the nation of Israel is tragic. Could Israel as a nation claim that its suffering had a purpose? Could their soul be a sin offering? By no means! Israel suffered for their sin. Only a sinless Messiah could suffer on behalf of others.

Yet it pleased Yahweh(*Jealous one*) to bruise him. He has caused him to suffer. When you make his soul an offering for sin, he will see his offspring. He will prolong his days, and the pleasure of Yahweh(*Jealous one*) will prosper in his hand. After the suffering of his soul, he will see the light and be satisfied. My righteous Servant will justify many by the knowledge of himself; and he will bear their iniquities. (Isaiah 53:10-11 TNT)

Jesus, the righteous Servant of Yahweh, bore the iniquity of the world. It pleased Yahweh to bruise Him because His suffering redeemed all humanity– everyone who would receive Jesus as Lord. This Servant is the one Yahweh raised up– as Peter referred to in the book of Acts:

God, having raised up his servant, Jesus, sent him to you first, to bless you, in turning away every one of you from your wickedness (Acts 3:26 ESV).

101

Chapter Thirty-Three

UNVEILED

There is a veil over the eyes of many Jews and Muslims concerning who our God is. Jesus will one day remove this veil from their eyes when they submit to Him as Lord. Paul writes:

But their minds were made dull, for to this day the same veil remains when the old covenant is read. It has not been removed, because only in Christ is it taken away. Even to this day when Moses is read, a veil covers their hearts.

(2 Corinthians 3:13-14 NIV)

Christ will take the veil away, but we must proclaim His name to them, so they will know He is the way, the truth, and the life. The veil is not removed in ceremony, tradition, or animal sacrifice. Nor is it removed with good intentions, church attendance, or acts of kindness. Only in Christ is the veil removed.

As Jesus breathed his last, hanging between heaven and earth on the cross, something supernatural happened. The gospel of Mark tells us: **"The veil of the temple was torn in two from the top to the bottom"** (Mark 15:38 WEB). This veil or curtain is what separates the Holy Place from the Holy of Holies in the temple. The ark of the covenant was located in the Holy of Holies, where Yahweh promised to meet with his people.

Put the altar in front of the curtain that shields the ark of the covenant law—before the atonement cover that is over the tablets of the covenant law—where I will meet with you.

(Exodus 30:6 NIV)

This curtain was massive, and some early Jewish traditions stated that the Temple veil was as thick as a man's hand. It was ripped from top to bottom when Jesus breathed his last. That which was hung was torn– both Jesus and the veil. Man did not open the way back to the Father because it would have been torn from the bottom up. Yahweh tore the veil to open the way for the world to return to Him through His precious Son, Jesus. Let the veil be torn!

MANY OF THE JEWS IN THE TIME OF JESUS HAD ATTAINED A SYSTEM OF RIGHTEOUSNESS THAT WAS VERY DIFFICULT TO ACHIEVE. JESUS CAME TO EXPOSE THE PRIDE OF WORKS– DRIVEN SALVATION. ISRAEL, AS A NATION, STUMBLED IN THE 1ST CENTURY AND MISSED THE MESSIAH BECAUSE OF THIS PRIDE. BUT THEY HAVE NOT STUMBLED BEYOND RECOVERY. "HAVE THEY STUMBLED THAT THEY SHOULD FALL? GOD FORBID: BUT RATHER THROUGH THEIR FALL SALVATION IS COME UNTO THE GENTILES, FOR TO PROVOKE THEM TO JEALOUSY." (ROMANS 11:11 KING JAMES VERSION)

Chapter Thirty-Four

YAHWEH SAVES

The Book of Revelation calls Jesus in His exalted position, "the Lamb of God." The crowds of heaven cry out, **"Salvation belongs to our God, who sits on the throne, and to the Lamb"** (Revelation 7:10). Yahweh and the Lamb joined together in bringing salvation to humankind. **"The throne of God and of the Lamb will be in it..."** (Revelations 22:3 ESV) reminds us that the throne sits two or there are two thrones. This idea is echoed in the book of Daniel: **"As I looked, thrones were placed, and the Ancient of Days took his seat"** (Daniel 7:9 ESV). The Father-Son narrative takes shape in this Old Testament apocalyptic writing. The ancient Jews studied the book of Daniel to understand the end times, much like Christians today study the book of Revelation. The plan of redemption would be accomplished through a Father and Son effort.

Though Jesus is usually the one we consider the Savior, Yahweh is also noted as a Savior throughout the Bible. **"For I am Yahweh your God, the Holy One of Israel, your Savior"** (Isaiah 43:3 WEB). And again, Isaiah writes, **"I, even I, am Yahweh; and besides me there is no Savior"** (Isaiah 43:11 WEB). And once more, he writes: **"All flesh shall know that I, Yahweh, am your Savior, and your Redeemer, the Mighty One of Jacob"** (Isaiah 49:26 WEB).

The name of Jesus or Yeshua means "Yahweh will save" and speaks to the purpose for which Jesus came to the planet. The verb in the name Yeshua is SHUA which means *"salvation, deliverance, protection, often implying a victory is at hand."*[27] Included also in the name of Yeshua is the name of YAH, which is the nickname for Yahweh.

The two powers of heaven worked together to save you and me. The kingdom of God works because a Father and Son desired to rescue us and bring us victory. A Savior sent a Savior to be born on earth and to take his seat as the new king. In doing so, Jesus fulfilled a prophecy written over 700 years earlier. A virgin would give birth. Isaiah prophecies: **"Behold, the virgin shall conceive and bear a son, and shall call his name Immanuel."** (Isaiah 7:14 ESV).

The name Immanuel means, "Our God with us." His name is not Immanuyah, meaning, "Yahweh is with us." When theologians say that our God came in the flesh, we think of Yahweh himself coming to earth. But instead, it is his Son Jesus, who also claims the title of God, and He came in the flesh.

"GOD BECAME MAN THAT MAN MIGHT BECOME GOD" ATHANASIUS (CA 298–373)

---

[27] Strong's Concordance, *shua*

Chapter Thirty-Five

MODALISM

Most Christians fail to separate the persons of the Trinity and clearly distinguish between the Father and the Son. Without this distinction, many inadvertently fall into a heresy called "modalism." Modalism is a belief that one God operates in different modes at different times.

To make the stance that there are two powers in heaven allows us to clear up the muddied waters that the Trinity creates. A Father and Son who co-rule throughout eternity is the narrative the Jews understood in the 1st Century. Yahweh usually assumed the title "God" throughout the Bible, and Jesus most often bears the title "Lord." Reading through the book of Acts shows the earliest disciples identifying Jesus as Lord (over 25 times in the book of Acts). Accepting the notion of two powers in heaven allows us to easily separate the role of Yahweh and the role of Jesus. The earliest Christians did not believe Yahweh came to earth in the flesh; instead, He sent His Son. Jesus never claimed that He was Yahweh; instead, He proclaimed the His position as His Son. Look at Jesus's statement to the Jews:

I and the Father are one. The Jews picked up stones again to stone him. Jesus answered them, "I have shown you many good works from the Father; for which of them are you going to stone me?" (John 10:30-31 ESV)

106

Note here in John 10:30 that Jesus mentions that he and the Father are one. I believe the "one" Jesus refers to is the oneness of the covenant he has with the Father. Yahweh is a covenantal God reaching out to bring you and me into a relationship with Him through His Son Jesus. Jesus did not come making Himself God or claiming He was Yahweh:

The Jews answered him, "It is not for a good work that we are going to stone you but for blasphemy, because you, being a man, make yourself God." Jesus answered them, "Is it not written in your Law, 'I said, you are gods'? If he called them gods to whom the word of God came—and Scripture cannot be broken— do you say of him whom the Father consecrated and sent into the world, 'You are blaspheming,' because I said, 'I am the Son of God? (John 10:32-36 ESV)

Jesus' blasphemous statement was that He was Yahweh's unique Son, the coming power of heaven to earth. I have found that many Christians fail to separate Jesus from the Father. Yahweh did not come in the flesh– Jesus did. Jesus did not pray to himself– he prayed to his Father in heaven. If we accept there are two powers in heaven, we are embracing the predominant Jewish belief system during the time of Jesus.

In practice, I believe many Christians see the Creator operating this way. Like I can be a father, I can also be a son; the thought was that the God of the universe operated as a Father and a Son and a Spirit. This belief condemned as a heresy by Tertullian in 213 A.D.

Chapter Thirty-Six

LAMB FOREVER

By glorifying and recognizing Jesus, we honor the Father. The book of Revelation is a picture of men, purchased for God by the blood of Jesus, who are rejoicing exceedingly around the throne. We are spectacularly favored by a God who is highly gracious! The foundation of our praise must be based upon Jesus' great sacrifice for us.

Scholars have discovered first eleven chapters of Genesis are the storyline behind the development of many of the primary characters of the Chinese language. I believe that after the scattering following the Tower of Babel, a group left Babel and headed east toward what is now China. Their language was based upon the ideas they held in common before they left Babel.

For instance, the Chinese character for "to covet or desire" combines of a picture of woman and a picture of two trees.[27] Chinese culture and the Bible relate sheep to *personal* sacrifice and redemption. These attributes are similar to God's sacrificial Lamb: the Lord Jesus Christ.

©www.Bible.ca

義 = 羊 + 我 (手 + 戈)

| Righteousness | Sheep | Me | Hand | Knife |

The character that means "righteousness" in Chinese consists of a sheep placed on top of 'me' and suggests that each individual has to make a personal choice to gain righteousness through the sacrificial sheep.

When we perceive righteousness as our own doing, we often become complacent in our worship. Complacency is a feeling of smug or uncritical satisfaction with oneself or one's achievements. Many churches lack passion in their relationship with Jesus because they feel they have attained righteousness. Complacency is the brother of self-righteousness.

True righteousness is trusting in the work that Jesus did to save us and bring us into relationship with our God. The world will become happy when we worship our God and the Lamb!

There will be no curse anymore. The throne of God and of the Lamb will be in it, and his servants serve him. They will see his face, and his name will be on their foreheads (Revelation 22:3-4 ESV).

Happiness in the Chinese language is the character for our God and the character for sheep combined!

©www.Bible.ca

| Happiness | God | Sheep |

This ancient culture understood that we could not be reconciled to our Creator without sacrifice. Why is Jesus called the Lamb?

A lamb is an animal a Jew would sacrifice for his sin. The lamb is also the animal that was sacrificed during the feast of Passover. We overcome by the blood of the Lamb (Revelation 12:12), and for eternity we will be reminded that Jesus gave His life for us. We will join the chorus of heaven, singing,

Worthy is the Lamb, who was slain, to receive power and wealth and wisdom and strength and honor and glory and praise. (Revelation 5:12 NIV)

The Book of Revelation distinguishes between the throne of God and the throne of the Lamb. God Yahweh is an individual. Jesus is an individual. To be an individual means that you cannot be divided into another.[28]

BISHOP ATHANASIUS, WHO LIVED IN THE 4ᵀᴴ CENTURY, HAD COME TO THE CONCLUSION THAT MANY OPPOSED THE NICENE CREED BECAUSE THEY FEARED THAT THE ASSERTION THAT THE SON WAS OF THE SAME SUBSTANCE AS THE FATHER COULD BE UNDERSTOOD AS MEANING THAT THERE IS NO DISTINCTION BETWEEN THE FATHER AND THE SON.

---

[28] late Middle English (in the sense 'indivisible'): from medieval Latin *individualis*, from Latin *individuus*, from *in-* 'not' + *dividuus* 'divisible' (from *dividere* 'to divide', Oxford Dictionary

Chapter Thirty-Seven

CHOOSE A LAMB DAY

The celebration of Palm Sunday is the beginning time of preparation for Passover, which is one of the most important holy days for the Jewish people. Passover celebrated their ancestors' emancipation from Egypt, made possible through the blood of lambs on their houses.

Jesus chose to enter Jerusalem on a specific day, four days before his death, for a reason. The day He entered Jerusalem was the time that each Jewish family chose a lamb for their household.

Tell all the congregation of Israel that on the tenth day of this month every man shall take a lamb according to their fathers' houses, a lamb for a household. (Exodus 12:3 NIV)

Each Jewish household would then examine the lamb for four days to be sure that this lamb had no blemish or defect.

Jesus entered Jerusalem on "Palm Sunday." He desired that the nation of Israel would choose Him as their lamb. When John the Baptist saw Jesus, he said, **"Behold, the Lamb of God, who takes away the sin of the world"** (John 1:29). Jesus was born to be the Passover lamb who would take away our sin. When He rode into Jerusalem four days before his death, there was great excitement! The crowds shouted, **"Blessed is the king**

111

who comes in the name of the Lord! Peace in heaven and glory in the highest!" (Luke 19:38 NIV).

Sadly, the same crowd that cheered Him on this day was shouting "Crucify Him!" four days later. They cheered Jesus because He seemingly fit into their theology, plan of redemption, and cultural preferences. On Palm Sunday, Jesus wept over Jerusalem, saying, **"Would that you, even you, had known on this day the things that make for peace!"** (Luke 19:42 NIV). The Jewish people wanted a ruler to deliver them, not a lamb to die for them.

It is no coincidence that Jesus was arrested, condemned, and crucified during the feast of Passover. Jesus modeled what every Passover lamb experienced from Palm Sunday to the crucifixion. He shows up in Jerusalem, inviting the Jews to choose him as their lamb for their household. Taking a lamb was commanded since the first Passover.

Tell all the congregation of Israel that on the tenth day of this month every man shall take a lamb. Your lamb shall be without blemish, a male a year old. You shall keep it until the fourteenth day of this month, when the whole assembly of the congregation of Israel shall kill their lambs at twilight.
(Exodus 12:5-6 NIV)

Jesus arrived in Jerusalem on Choose a Lamb Day, the tenth of Nisan. We call it Palm Sunday, but to the Jews, every family would find a lamb for their household. Over the next four days, the family would live with the lamb to be sure it was without blemish.

The Jewish leadership questioned Jesus after arriving on Palm Sunday. **"Now while the Pharisees were gathered together, Jesus asked them a question"** (Matthew 22:41). They desired to trap or discredit him. **"Then the Pharisees went and plotted how to entangle him in his words"** (Matthew 22:15). After four days of inspecting Jesus with their questions, the Bible tells us: **"And no one was able to answer him a word, nor from that day did anyone dare to ask him any more questions"** (Matthew 22:46). The Jewish leaders were left speechless and convinced that words alone could not stop this man. He had to be killed because he was without blemish.

Just as the Passover lamb had to be judged without blemish, so Jesus was also deemed innocent by six other witnesses. Only a lamb without blemish could be an acceptable sacrifice. And only this lamb's blood could be placed upon the doorpost of the households.

1. Judas Iscariot: **"I have sinned by betraying innocent blood."** (Matthew 27:4).

2. Pontius Pilate: **"Then Pilate said to the chief priests and the crowds, 'I find no guilt in this man.'"** (Luke 23:4).

3. Herod Antipas: **"He sent him back to us. Look, nothing deserving death has been done by him"** (Luke 23:15).

4. Pontius Pilate's Wife: **"Have nothing to do with that righteous man, for I have suffered much because of him today in a dream."** (Matthew 27:19).

5. Dying Thief: **"And we indeed justly, for we are receiving the due reward of our deeds; but this man has done nothing wrong"** (Luke 23:41).

6. Roman Centurion: **"Now when the centurion saw what had taken place, he praised God, saying, 'Certainly this man was innocent!'"** (Luke 23:47).

BACK IN THE 1800'S IN SAN FRANCISCO, THERE WERE TWO BROTHERS WHO MOVED INTO A VIOLENT AREA. THE YOUNGER BROTHER DECIDED TO GET INVOLVED WITH A BUNCH OF THUGS AND IN TIME ENDED UP IN A KNIFE FIGHT IN WHICH HE MURDERED ANOTHER MAN. AS HE FLED THE SCENE, HE RAN INTO HIS HOUSE AND UP INTO HIS ROOM, THROWING HIS BLOODY CLOTHES ON THE FLOOR AND HIDING IN THE CLOSET. THE NEXT THING HE HEARD WAS SOMEONE COMING UP THE STAIRS, THEN SOMEONE BREAKING DOWN THE DOOR, AND THEN COMMOTION, FOLLOWED BY TOTAL SILENCE. AFTER A FEW MOMENTS, HE CAME OUT OF THE CLOSET, ONLY TO REALIZE THAT HIS BIG BROTHER HAD PUT ON HIS BLOOD-SOAKED SHIRT AND WAS TAKEN AWAY BY THE POLICE TO BE PUT TO DEATH FOR HIS YOUNGER BROTHER'S CRIME.

Chapter Thirty-Eight

HANDLE THE BLOOD

Passover is a special holy day in that each household learns how to handle the blood for their own family. Scriptures forbade anyone not ordained as a priest to make blood sacrifices.

And you shall say to them, 'Any one of the house of Israel, or of the strangers who sojourn among them, who offers a burnt offering or sacrifice and does not bring it to the entrance of the tent of meeting to offer it to the LORD, that man shall be cut off from his people.'(Leviticus 17:8-9 ESV)

Yet the first Passover required each household to take a lamb, inspect it, sacrifice it, and place its blood upon their own house.

Passover reminds us that all those with blemishes cannot be sacrificed. The blood of those lambs would not keep out the angel of death. Only through the blood of an unblemished lamb can a household be protected.

Jesus was declared without blemish by the priesthood, the government, and the people. On Passover, all blemished lambs go free, and all unblemished lambs die. This is true for us: all of us with sin can go free on the day that the innocent one is condemned to death.

The Old Testament creates a narrative or a story that prepares us for the coming of Jesus Christ, the Son of God.

115

Passover points to the Lamb that will forever sit on the throne of his Father in heaven.

Today's church overlooks the message of Passover, but the early church did not. One of the earliest sects of Christianity called themselves the "Quartodecimans" or "fourteeners." The Fourteeners were so named because they celebrated Passover on the 14th day of the month of Nisan. Roman culture was already attempting to shift Christians away from their Jewish roots by changing the times of their celebrations. The Quartodecimans became a specific sect of Christians in hopes of never forgetting the importance of the Passover.

JEWISH TRADITION TELLS US THAT ON THE DAY OF PASSOVER, THE PRIEST WOULD GO INTO THE FIELD AND CUT DOWN THE FIRST-FRUITS PORTION OF THE HARVEST. PASSOVER IS THE FEAST DAY ON WHICH JESUS WAS CRUCIFIED. ONCE THE FIRST-FRUITS PORTION WAS CUT DOWN ON THE DAY OF PASSOVER, IT WOULD LIE THERE UNTIL THE DAY AFTER THE SABBATH. THE FEAST OF FIRST-FRUITS IS DESCRIBED IN LEVITICUS 23. CHRIST WAS CUT DOWN ON PASSOVER DAY AND LAY IN THE TOMB THREE DAYS AND THREE NIGHTS, ONLY TO BE RAISED UP ON THE DAY AFTER THE SABBATH.

Chapter Thirty-Nine

MARRY THE LAMB

During Passover, the Israelites were told to take a lamb and put its blood on the doorposts.

Then Moses(*Drawn out*) called for all the elders of Israel(*Struggles with God*) and said to them, "Drag away and take lambs according to your families, and kill the Passover."

(Exodus 12:1 TNT)

Through the blood of this innocent lamb, the Israelites were saved from death, and Yahweh entered their homes. The Hebrew translation of this verse in Exodus 12 has a much deeper meaning. Most translations say, "Go and select a lamb" but the words "drag away" and "take" carry imagery that I want to put into words. "Dragging away" a lamb can refer to something violently seized or purchased– the root word comes from the same root word as in the name of "Moses." Moses was drawn out or dragged out of the Nile River by the Egyptian princess— literally saved from drowning. The word for take in Hebrew is the same for taking a wife into marriage. Taking the lamb also implied marrying the lamb or coming into covenant with the lamb.

Let us rejoice and exult and give him the glory, for the marriage of the Lamb has come, and his Bride has made herself ready; it was granted her to clothe herself with fine

linen, bright and pure—for the fine linen is the righteous deeds of the saints. And the angel said to me, "Write this: Blessed are those who are invited to the marriage supper of the Lamb" (Revelation 19:7-9 ESV).

Notice also in the Hebrew text that the Lamb is the Passover– the text just says, "Kill the Passover," not the Passover lamb. The Lamb itself is the Passover. This same idea is repeated by the apostle Paul in the letter to the Corinthians.

Cleanse out the old leaven that you may be a new lump, as you really are unleavened. For Christ, our Passover lamb has been sacrificed (1 Corinthians 5:7 NIV)

The Greek text calls Jesus the Pascha or the Passover, not using the word lamb. The Passover is the Lamb, and Jesus is the Lamb of God. John ends the Bible with this picture.

Then the angel showed me the river of the water of life, as clear as crystal, flowing from the throne of God and of the Lamb. (Revelations 22:1 NIV)

Note that two powers now sit on one throne. There is a God, the title Yahweh takes throughout the Bible. There is also the Lamb, who is Jesus, the unique Son of God. He is called the Lamb because of the sacrifice He made to bring us into the family of God. The Lamb is the picture of the Passover Lamb whose blood was placed on the doorposts of the Israelites to spare them from the angel of death that was passing through Egypt. Jesus's protective and saving blood reminds us of our need for a Savior to have access to our God Himself. History unfolds as a king's son sacrifices himself to establish his father's kingdom on earth.

Chapter Forty

THE NEW KING

Many of us live with a democratic mindset instead of a kingdom mindset. A king in ancient times would establish his son upon his throne, thus beginning a new era throughout the kingdom. Jesus told His disciples, **"I tell you the truth, some who are standing here will not taste death before they see the kingdom of God come with power"** (Mark 9:1). Jesus wanted his disciples to have great anticipation about his inauguration. Let's begin by examining the meaning of dynasty and how this concept applies to the kingdom of God. The word *inaugurated* describes the beginning or introduction of a new policy or administration. The word describes the action of formally admitting someone to office.[29] The process of His inauguration is the event Jesus described to Peter, James, and John:

And Jesus was saying to them, "Truly I say to you, there are some of those who are standing here who will not taste death until they see the kingdom of God after it has come with power." (Mark 9:1 NAS)

This event was fulfilled when Jesus ascended to the throne. The outpouring of the Spirit signified the day the kingdom was officially opened to the public. The Day of Pentecost marked the

---

[29] Ehrlich, Eugene. *Oxford American Dictionary*. New York: Oxford UP, 1980.

establishment of the name of Jesus as the name above every other name, and that day was celebrated with the outpouring of the Spirit! The kingdom of heaven is released on earth when Christians begin to operate in the power of the Spirit.

About a hundred years after the church was established in the Roman empire, a fresh fire began to burn that was as powerful and controversial as the day of Pentecost. Montanism sprung up in the province of Asia Minor during the late 2nd century. It was named after its founder Montanus but was also known as the New Prophecy. This movement operated in signs and wonders, speaking in tongues and prophecy, and even had women in places of authority in their meetings. The famous early church father, Tertullian, became an adherent to this move of God.

Montanus sparked a great revival that was opposed by many in the church. Prophecy was being spoken and miracles were being performed. Many in the movement believed the Paraclete was being restored to the church as promised in the book of John. Montanus taught that the Paraclete was different from Jesus and the Holy Spirit– another entity to be experienced. But even though their beliefs were slightly off, their passion for the kingdom made history.

John Wesley, the founder of Methodism in the 18th century, wrote in his journal:

"I was fully convinced of what I had long suspected, that the Montanists, in the second and third centuries, were real, scriptural Christians; and that the grand reason why the miraculous gifts were

so soon withdrawn was not only that faith and holiness were well-
nigh lost; but that dry, formal, orthodox men began even then to
ridicule whatever gifts they had not themselves, and to decry them all
as either madness or imposture."[30]

Wesley described Montanus as a 'real scriptural Christian' and extolled him as 'one of the best men ever upon the earth.' The reason why speaking in tongues and similar gifts had disappeared, Wesley said, was that 'dry, formal, orthodox men' had begun to 'ridicule' such gifts because they themselves did not possess them.

One of the biggest challenges we have as Christians is dealing with persecution from religious people. We must embrace both the Scriptures and the power of our God, or we will be in error. Jesus said in Matthew 22:29, **"You are wrong, because you know neither the Scriptures nor the power of God."**

We live in a season which requires us to navigate with zeal and confidence mixed with the fear of the LORD and humility. Humble as lambs and bold as kings. Jesus was sacrificed as a lamb but rose as a king. We must live as lambs among wolves, and even lambs to the slaughter. But we are royal lambs with authority that flows from King Jesus.

---

[30] Commonplace Holiness Blog - Craig L. Adams.
https://craigladams.com/blog/john-wesley-and-spiritual-gifts/

Chapter Forty-One
MOVING AIR

As we discuss the spirit in this chapter, we find the most basic meaning of the word spirit is "moving air." This is why the word Spirit is *always* linked to breath or wind. The Greek word for spirit is *pneuma* and the word in Hebrew is *ruach*. Both words mean spirit, breath, or wind. *Pnuema* is the Greek word for spirit, wind or breath and is used interchangeably by translators depending on the context. *Pneumatos* is the Greek word for "of the Spirit, wind or breath." John 3 is a great example of how *pneuma* is translated differently based on the context.

"That which is born of the flesh is flesh, and that which is born of the Spirit*(pneumatos)* **is spirit***(pnuema)*. **Do not marvel that I said to you, 'You must be born again. The wind***(pneuma)* **blows where it wishes, and you hear its sound, but you do not know where it comes from or where it goes. So, it is with everyone who is born of the Spirit***(pneumatos)*.**"**

(John 3:6-8 ESV)

The Spirit and wind are described as blowing in this verse. The Greek word for blowing comes from the root word *pneo* meaning *"to move as wind with relatively rapid motion, blow"* or *"to emit an odor, breathe out."*[1] The verb connected with *pnuema* grounds us in the idea of air that is in motion either by blowing violently or

[1] Bauer/Danker *Greek-English Lexicon of the New Testament, pneo*

breathing softly.

It is important to note that the Council of Nicaea in 325 A.D., in response to the Arian controversy, came forth with a statement or creed that failed to identify the Holy Spirit as a separate person. Only in later creeds was the language included which declared the Spirit as a separate personality. The church was seemingly more aligned with asserting there were two powers in heaven than three.

WEATHER PATTERNS ARE LITERALLY POURED OUT INTO AN AREA LIKE WATER BEING POURED OUT INTO A BASIN. WHEN TWO WEATHER FRONTS COLLIDE, THERE IS USUALLY THUNDER AND LIGHTNING BEFORE THE ATMOSPHERE CHANGES. ONCE THE ATMOSPHERE IS POURED OUT, THE ENTIRE REGION IS CHANGED. WARM WEATHER REPLACES FRIGID AIR, OR VICE VERSA, AND LIFE ADJUSTS ACCORDINGLY. I BELIEVE THAT THE HOLY SPIRIT IS POURED OUT OVER AN AREA IN THE SAME WAY. LITERALLY THE SPIRIT OF GOD COMES INTO A REGION AND SHIFTS THE ENTIRE ATMOSPHERE. "FOR I WILL POUR WATER ON THE THIRSTY LAND, AND STREAMS ON THE DRY GROUND; I WILL POUR OUT MY SPIRIT ON YOUR OFFSPRING, AND MY BLESSING ON YOUR DESCENDANTS" (ISAIAH 44:3).

Chapter Forty-Two

FLESH AND SPIRIT

Jesus contrasts the flesh and the spirit. As the flesh is of a person, so the spirit is of a person. As the flesh would not be its own person, neither would the spirit be its own person. The Bible often speaks of the flesh and the spirit as in opposition. Jesus said, **"It is the Spirit which gives life. The flesh profits nothing."** (John 6:63 TNT).

Throughout Scripture, the Spirit will be connected with things such as fire, water, or the flesh. John writes, **"...the Spirit and the water and the blood; and these three agree"** (1 John 5:8). Usually when making comparisons, we would compare a table to a chair, or Mary to Kim. The gospel compares fire and the Holy Spirit– a baptism into two different things, Spirit and fire. Matthew spoke of the Messiah, that **"He will baptize you with the Holy Spirit and fire"** (Matthew 3:11 KJV). The Spirit is compared to water, blood, and fire and not three other people. We are baptized into something, not baptized into a person. Much of the imagery points to the Spirit which flows from the person of Jesus or the Father.

In Matthew and Mark, evil spirits are referred to as "unclean spirits." When people do evil things and have evil thoughts, they become unclean and attract the spirit of uncleanness. The opposite holds true for those who pursue

125

righteousness. They become inhabited by the spirit of holiness (i.e., the Holy Spirit). Demonic possession needs to be encountered with Holy Spirit possession. A spirit is either holy or unclean, from the kingdom of God or from the kingdom of darkness. We are breathing in good air or bad air, a good spirit, or a bad spirit. Evil spirits are like viruses that infect us and how we think and feel. The chart below is a diagram of how we might understand the spirit realm.

Father and Son

Kingdom of Light
Angels and Heavenly Beings
Life   holy
SPIRIT
Death   unclean
demons
Kingdom of Darkness

Satan

The word for holiness in Hebrew is *kadosh*. The Hebrew word *kadosh* signifies an act or state in which people or things are set aside and reserved exclusively for God. They must be withheld from ordinary use and treated with exceptional care as something which belongs to God.

We have the Spirit of holiness– not because we are more

righteous than others. We receive the Holy Spirit because we are set apart for our God through Jesus. Jews understood one must separate not only between what is evil and good but also what is common and what is holy. Christians live their lives as a people belonging to our God. Yahweh told Moses: **"You must distinguish between the holy and the common, between the unclean and the clean"** (Leviticus 10:10 NIV). Moses was to teach the Israelites the difference between holy and common; clean and unclean. Our actions will determine the spirit in which we live. The Holy Spirit is the spirit given to those who are set apart for the kingdom of our God. When we occupy our lives with religious activities and thoughts, we are filled with the Holy Spirit. When we fill our lives with unclean actions and ideas, we become contaminated with an unclean spirit.

BREATHING AND SPEAKING GIVE US A PICTURE OF HOW OUR WORDS ARE CARRIERS OF SPIRIT. I CAN REMEMBER TEACHING MY CHILDREN THIS CONCEPT ONE DAY. I HAD THEM PUT THEIR HANDS IN FRONT OF THEIR MOUTHS AS THEY WERE SPEAKING. I TOLD THEM TO NOTICE AS THEY SPOKE HOW THEY COULD FEEL THE PUFFS OF AIR COMING OUT WITH THE WORDS. WORDS ARE EMPOWERED BY BREATH AND CARRY CREATIVE OR DAMAGING POWER WITHIN THEM.

Chapter Forty-Three

NOT A GHOST

The King James Version translates the word for spirit, *pneuma*, as "ghost." This famous translation, written in 1611, promoted a 'Holy Ghost' instead of a "Holy Spirit." The King James Version translation of ghost implies a separate personality instead of the breath of someone.

There is a word for ghost in the Greek language. The word for spirit, *pneuma,* should never be translated as "ghost'" The term for *phantom* in the Greek language describes a ghost. A ghost is defined in the Oxford Dictionary as "an apparition of a dead person which is believed to appear or become manifest to the living."[2]

The gospel of Matthew tells us about the disciples seeing Jesus walking on water while crossing the Lake of Galilee. The Greek word *phantom* refers to Jesus as a ghost and not the word pnuema:

When the disciples saw him walking on the lake, they were terrified. 'It's a ghost,' they said, and cried out in fear.

(Matthew 14:26 NIV)

Below is a graph that shows acceptable translations of the word spirit in the Bible:

[2] Ehrlich, Eugene. *Oxford American Dictionary*. New York: Oxford UP, 1980.

Acceptable Translations

Greek pnuema
Hebrew ruach

WIND ✓

BREATH ✓

SPIRIT ✓

~~GHOST~~

Unacceptable Translations

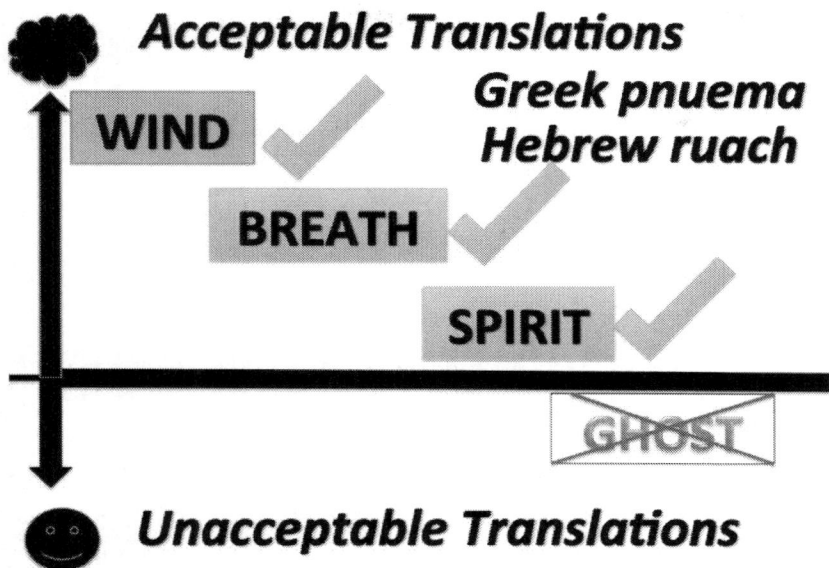

Referring to 'the Holy Spirit' as 'the Holy Ghost' is not a good interpretation. A ghost infers a separate person other than Jesus and Yahweh, but the Bible teaches that the Spirit originates from them.

THE VERY NATURE OF WATER WILL TAKE THE SHAPE OF THE VESSEL INTO WHICH IT IS POURED. THE SPIRIT IN US TAKES THE SHAPE OF WHO WE WERE MEANT TO BE. THE SPIRIT OVER US BRINGS US TOGETHER INTO ONE BODY LIKE LIQUID JESUS FLOWING IN US AND OVER US. "FOR WE WERE ALL BAPTIZED BY ONE SPIRIT INTO ONE BODY, AND WE WERE ALL GIVEN THE ONE SPIRIT TO DRINK." (1 CORINTHIANS 12:13)

Chapter Forty-Four

NO NAME

In 1972, *Horse With No Name* became a hit and went all the way to No. 1 on the U.S. Billboard Hot 100 chart. The famous line in the song was, *"I've been through the desert on a horse with no name."* Yes! It is odd that the horse has no name. That is the same question I have asked about the Holy Spirit– where is the name?

Consider that the first act of Adam was to name the animals. Think about the times in Scripture when someone had an angelic encounter, and they responded, "What is your name!" The meaning of names in the Bible, whether of people, places, or events–carries great significance. We know this because certain passages explain the meaning of the name and its importance to the reader.   For instance, the apostle Paul reminded Philemon of the significance of his runaway slave when he included the meaning of the slave's name, Onesimus, in his letter. Onesimus means "useful." So, the text actually reads as follows:

Onesimus(*Useful*) who became my son while I was in chains. Formerly he was useless to you, but now he has become useful both to you and to me (Philemon 1:10-11 NIV).

Paul wrote that Onesimus was useful, just as his name foretold. (Although Philemon probably needed some convincing of that fact.) Paul connected the meaning of Onesimus's name purposefully to provide hope, encouragement, and direction to the situation.

In ancient Hebraic thought, when something is named, it is then aligned with its purpose and existence. To not give a name to something or someone is a denial of its individual existence. Imagine if you went to someone's house and they had five children. The children were named John, Fred, Annie, Mary, and Good Boy. As you engage with the children, every time you greet Good Boy, you wonder why the parents didn't give this child a real name. There is something missing about this child because he was given a title or nickname but not a real name.

Some say that Holy is the name of the Spirit. Yet Scripture identifies the Holy Spirit also as the Spirit of God, the Spirit of Christ, and the Spirit of the LORD. I would conclude that holy is its purpose, not its name.

IN THE BOOK OF ACTS, THERE IS NOT ONE TIME THE DISCIPLES BAPTIZED 'IN THE NAME OF THE FATHER AND OF THE SON AND OF THE HOLY SPIRIT.' BEING JESUS' FINAL INSTRUCTIONS BEFORE ASCENDING TO HEAVEN, HOW COULD THE DISCIPLES HAVE MISUNDERSTOOD? EITHER THE DISCIPLES WERE DIRECTLY DISOBEDIENT TO JESUS, OR JESUS NEVER USED THIS METHOD OF BAPTISM.

Chapter Forty-Five

SEPARATE PERSON?

The most personal way we can experience the Father and the Son is by his Spirit or his breath. When you feel someone else's breath, you are very close to them! The eyes of the LORD or the arm of the LORD are fully possessed by the LORD, as is the Spirit of the LORD. When the Bible refers to the spirit of Elijah, we understand that it refers to his life and influence being renewed in others. When the Lord releases His Spirit on us, He is not releasing another person. His Spirit is His influence, and life is poured out over us. The Spirit in the lungs of Yahweh is breathed into our lungs.

Jesus quotes Isaiah 61 declaring the Spirit of Yahweh is on me: **"The Lord Yahweh's Spirit is on me, because Yahweh has anointed me to preach good news to the humble"** (Isaiah 61:1 WEB). Yahweh anoints Jesus to preach the good news, as quoted in Luke 4:18. The Spirit of Yahweh is upon Jesus because Yahweh anointed Jesus. We are able to receive His Spirit when we humble ourselves before Him.

Yahweh(*Jealous one*) said, "My Spirit will not strive with man forever, because he is also flesh; so, his days will be one hundred twenty years." (Genesis 6:3 TNT)

Would Yahweh say: "My Jesus will not strive?" Is Yahweh referring to His Spirit or the Holy Spirit? I would conclude that His Spirit is the Holy Spirit– not another person of the Godhead.

For the eyes of the LORD run to and fro throughout the whole earth, to give strong support to those whose heart is blameless toward him. (1 Chronicles 16:9 NIV)

The use of the word "eyes" in this text is the way the word "spirit" is used in the Bible. The eyes are of the LORD, not some separate personality. Nor would we consider the arm of the LORD as its own person. The book of Isaiah says: **"Who has believed our message? and to whom has the arm of Yahweh been revealed?"** (Isaiah 53:1 WEB).

Psalm 29 is all about the voice of the LORD.

The voice of the LORD is over the waters; the God of glory thunders, the LORD, over many waters. The voice of the LORD is powerful; the voice of the LORD is full of majesty. (Psalm 29:3-4 ESV)

The voice of the LORD is the audible influence of Yahweh over the world. The voice of the LORD thunders, and is powerful, and is full of majesty just like the Spirit of the LORD is! The voice of Yahweh is an extension of his person that we can experience and not its own entity. The breath of God restored life to Jesus, raising him from the dead and now lives in us!

And if the Spirit of him who raised Jesus from the dead is living in you, he who raised Christ from the dead will also give life to your mortal bodies through his Spirit, who lives in you. (Romans 8:11 NIV)

Seeing the Holy Spirit as another person with which we interact causes many Christians to ignore Jesus. I think we need to embrace the Holy Spirit as our Jesus Connection instead of placing some other mediator between our God and us. Jesus alone is our mediator, but the mysterious nature of the Holy Spirit ought to be fully pursued and activated in our lives.

IN BUSINESS, WE ALWAYS WANT TO ELIMINATE THE "MIDDLE-MAN". THE MIDDLEMAN DRIVES UP EXPENSES SO THAT WE WANT TO GO DIRECTLY TO THE SOURCE. IN AMERICA THERE IS A HUGE DEBATE OVER THE COST OF MEDICAL INSURANCE. INSURANCE IS SUPPOSED TO BE A MEDIATOR BETWEEN OUR SOURCE OF HEALTH AND US. BUT THE COST OF MEDICAL INSURANCE ALONE CAN MAKE US SICK!

YET ON THE OTHER HAND, A MEDIATOR IN SOME SITUATIONS IS THE ONLY WAY A CONFLICT CAN BE RESOLVED. MANY PEOPLE TODAY ARE TRYING TO ELIMINATE THE "MIDDLE-MAN" OUT OF THEIR SPIRITUAL LIFE. THEY WANT TO GO DIRECTLY TO GOD. THE PROBLEM IS THAT GOING DIRECTLY TO GOD WITHOUT JESUS CHRIST IS A SURE WAY TO DIE! JESUS FULFILLED THE TERMS OF THE COVENANT THAT GOD DEMANDED. A GOOD MEDIATOR WAS THE ONLY SOLUTION.

Chapter Forty-Six

OF FATHER AND SON

The reason we should always pray for more of the Holy Spirit is that we get more of Jesus and the Father when we do. We should not view the Holy Spirit as some impersonal force but nor should we view it as a separate person other than Jesus or the Father.

The Holy Spirit is described as a person in most people's theology who came in place of Jesus to walk with us and point us to the Father and the Son. But throughout the Old Testament and in the New Testament, the Holy Spirit is upon the earth. **For in one Spirit we were all baptized into one body—Jews or Greeks, slaves or free—and all were made to drink of one Spirit** (1 Corinthians 12:13 NIV).

We are not baptized into a person, nor do we drink of a person. We are baptized in water and drink water– something, not someone. We would be Biblically errant to emphasize the Holy Spirit as a separate person outside of Jesus and the Father. A simple reading of the eleven greetings found in the New Testament letters reveals that two powers, not just one or not three, are always acknowledged.[3]

---

[3] 2 Corinthians 1:2; Galatians 1:3; Ephesians 1:2; Philippians 1:2; Philemon 1:3; Colossians 1:3; 1 Thessalonians 1:1; 1 Timothy 1:2; 2 Timothy 1:2; 1 Peter 1:3

Grace to you and peace from God our Father and the Lord Jesus Christ (1 Corinthians 1:3 ESV).

The Spirit is not a separate person of the Trinity, but instead is the person of the Father or the Son. The opinion of this author is that the Holy Spirit is the Spirit of our God or of Christ and is not its own person. If the Holy Spirit was its own individual person, it would have been given a name. The Holy Spirit is never once named in the Bible because the Spirit is of Yahweh or of Jesus.

The Name Translation Bible Project has caused me to clarify the difference between a title and a name. In the Hebrew Bible, you will read the name of Yahweh about 6,000 times, yet most translations use the title 'LORD" instead of His name. Failing to clarify the difference will hinder our ability to translate accurately.

"GOD" IS A TITLE, NOT A NAME. FORTY-SIX TIMES "GOD YAHWEH" APPEARS IN THE BIBLE. "GOD" REFERS TO HIS TITLE AND "YAHWEH" REFERS TO HIS NAME. THIS IS SIMILAR TO HOW WE WOULD READ ABOUT KING DAVID IN WHICH "KING" IS HIS TITLE AND "DAVID" IS HIS NAME. IN THE NEW TESTAMENT AS WE READ ABOUT CHRIST JESUS, "CHRIST" IS HIS TITLE AND "JESUS" IS HIS NAME.

Chapter Forty-Seven

BAPTISMAL NAME

The baptismal formula in Matthew 28:19, "baptizing them in the name of the Father and of the Son and of the Holy Spirit," is clear evidence of early usage of the threefold confession. Other early writings like the Didache also have this threefold confession. There are a few problems with including this phrase in the Bible.

1. The disciples practiced in the book of Acts only baptizing in the name of Jesus.

2. The Holy Spirit is never named in the Scriptures.

3. The names of the Father and the Son are different.

4. Early church historian Eusebius quotes Matthew 28:19 without the threefold confession in his writings prior to the 1st council of Nicaea.[4]

5. All other gospels refer to the name of Jesus

6. Every matter established by two or three witnesses

7. The Shem Tov reading of the book of Matthew in Hebrew lacks "in the name of the Father, and the Son and the Holy Spirit."

---

[4] The original form of Matthew 28:19 did not have the Trinitarian baptismal formula was the conclusion of F. C. Conybeare, "The Eusebian Form of the Text of Mt. 28:19," *ZNW* 2 (1901): 275-88

The addition of the Holy Spirit, as a separate person to be worshipped like the Father and the Son, was enforced at the Council of Constantinople in 381 A.D. Unlike the two powers of heaven that were embraced by the earliest Christians, the addition of this third power brought a new source of dispute amongst church leaders.[5] I believe the Holy Spirit is the most personal way we can experience the Father and the Son. When you feel someone else's breath, you are very close to them! But I also see many people praying and talking to the Holy Spirit instead of talking to the Father and Jesus.

Matthew 28:19 seems to incorporate the idea that the Father, Son, and Spirit all have the same name. Yet Scripture defines the Father's name as Yahweh, Son's name is Jesus, and the Holy Spirit is unnamed.

Interestingly, Matthew 28:19 was also the source of great debate in the early Pentecostal movement. The 1906 Asuza Street Revival, which I consider the Third Great Awakening, was a revival fire that spread worldwide. At a camp meeting in 1913, the Jesus Only movement or the Oneness Pentecostal movement was birthed based on the revelation that Jesus is the "name of the Father, Son, and the Holy Spirit." At this point, there was a schism between the Trinitarians and the Oneness Pentecostals.

---

[5] *A new source of dispute, too, was introduced by the requirement to accept the consubstantiality of the Holy Spirit.* Frend, William, H.C. The Early Church (p. 166). Kindle Edition.

Many believers were then rebaptized in the name of Jesus instead of the Trinitarian formula.

In the Pentecostal movement today, we have "Oneness" Pentecostals or "Jesus Only" Christians, who claim that Jesus is the Father, the Son, and the Spirit. We also have those from that period who stayed "Trinitarian," such as the Assemblies of God. I believe both views are orthodox because Jesus is treated like the Father. Though both ideas have a high Christology, neither view captures the real Biblical narrative that there are two powers in heaven.

WHY WOULD WE PRAY IN THE NAME OF JESUS, HEAL IN THE NAME OF JESUS, CAST OUT DEMONS IN HIS NAME, YET BAPTIZE IN THE NAME OF THE FATHER AND THE SON AND THE HOLY SPIRIT? IF JESUS COMMANDED HIS DISCIPLES TO BAPTIZE IN THE NAME 'OF THE FATHER, AND THE SON AND THE HOLY SPIRIT,' CLEARLY THAT COMMAND WOULD HAVE BEEN OBEYED BY THE EARLY DISCIPLES. PAUL WROTE THAT, "...WHATSOEVER YE DO IN WORD OR DEED, DO ALL IN THE NAME OF THE LORD JESUS..." (COLOSSIANS 3:17) THE NEW TESTAMENT IS A MESSAGE POINTING PEOPLE TO GOD'S SON, JESUS. HE IS SEATED AT THE RIGHT HAND OF THE FATHER WITH ALL AUTHORITY IN HEAVEN AND ON EARTH!

Chapter Forty-Eight

FIRST MENTION

Most Christians have been taught that the person of the Holy Spirit arrived on planet earth on the day of Pentecost. Jesus told his disciples:

But you will receive power when the Holy Spirit has come upon you; and you shall be My witnesses both in Jerusalem, and in all Judea and Samaria, and even to the remotest part of the earth (Acts 1:8 ESV)

We then see this fulfillment in the next chapter as the Jews gather for the Feast of Pentecost. This festival celebrates the giving of the Ten Commandments and the Mosaic Covenant at Mount Sinai. The feast of Pentecost is when Yahweh married Israel. Acts 2 is a picture of Jesus marrying the church.

When the day of Pentecost had come, they were all together in one place. And suddenly there came from heaven a noise like a violent rushing wind, and it filled the whole house where they were sitting. And there appeared to them tongues as of fire distributing themselves, and they rested on each one of them. And they were all filled with the Holy Spirit and began to speak with other tongues, as the Spirit was giving them utterance (Acts 2:1-4 NASB)

But prior to Pentecost we find the activity of the Holy Spirit. If the Holy Spirit was not already on the planet, how could Jesus breathe the Spirit upon them? **"And when He had said this, He breathed on them and said to them, 'Receive the Holy Spirit'"** (John 20:22 NIV). A closer look at the Bible reveals the Holy Spirit has been here since the book of Genesis.

"The earth was formless and void, and darkness was over the surface of the deep, and the Spirit of God was moving over the surface of the waters" (Genesis 1:2 NIV).

We also see the first time in the Scriptures where the Spirit of God comes upon someone by the name of "Bezalel," which means the shadow of God.

I have filled him with the Spirit of God in wisdom, in understanding, in knowledge, and in all kinds of craftsmanship. (Exodus 31:3 NIV)

King David cried out in the Psalms because of his sin, **"Take not your Holy Spirit from me"** (Psalm 51:11 NIV). Before his sinful actions, David lived a life full of the Holy Spirit. The Bible says the Spirit of God rushed over him as he was appointed King.

Then Samuel took the horn of oil and anointed him in the midst of his brothers. And the Spirit of the LORD rushed upon David from that day forward. (1 Samuel 16:13 NIV)

Early in the New Testament, we see the Spirit moving upon John the Baptist as he was in the womb of his mother Elizabeth:

When Elizabeth heard Mary's greeting, the baby leaped in her womb; and Elizabeth was filled with the Holy Spirit. (Luke 1:41 NIV)

Jesus Himself was full of the Holy Spirit after returning from His immersion and receiving the Father's blessing. **"Jesus, full of the Holy Spirit, returned from the Jordan and was led around by the Spirit in the wilderness"** (Luke 4:1 NIV). Jesus was full of the Holy Spirit and not in a relationship with the Holy Spirit. **"The Holy Spirit descended on him in bodily form"** (Luke 3:22 ESV). Jesus experienced the Spirit of God in His physical body. The Greek word for bodily form σωματικός (somatikos) is the same word used to describe physical or bodily training in 1 Timothy 4:8. You and I become partakers in the divine nature of our God when we encounter the Holy Spirit (2 Peter 1:3). The Spirit of our God breathed upon us imparts to us nature of our God. This process is called *theosis*– from the Greek word *theo* meaning God.

Assuming a person called "Holy Spirit" came at Pentecost is not congruent with the rest of the Bible. The mysteries of the Spirit in our lives should leave us in awe and wonder. Yahweh and Jesus breathe on us, and we are changed. We may never fully understand the mysterious ways of the Spirit of our God until we see Jesus face to face. As we immerse ourselves in His Spirit, we experience that reality that we are justified, sanctified, and glorified. The Holy Spirit in us allows us to encounter and feel Jesus and the Father intimately and powerfully.

THEOSIS IS SHARING IN THE DIVINE NATURE OF GOD.

Chapter Forty-Nine

GENDER BENDER

There is no text in the NT that clearly or even probably affirms the personality of the Holy spirit through the route of Greek grammar.[1]
Dr. Daniel Wallace, Professor of New Testament Studies at Dallas Theological Seminary

Rules of grammar play an important issue when developing doctrine. Translators are limited to the rules of grammar when making decisions about a translation. We cannot change the rules of grammar to confirm our theology. This chapter will go into detail about how translators are using masculine pronouns when referring to the Holy Spirit when in fact, the pronouns used for the Holy Spirit in the Greek New Testament are neuter. This conclusion is based upon the Greek text and not on any translation. The translators of the King James Version of the Bible correctly translated the pronoun for the Spirit as "itself."

The Spirit itself beareth witness with our spirit, that we are the children of God. (Romans 8:16 KJV)

Sadly, almost all other translations mistranslate the pronoun to *Himself* instead of *itself*. Translators mistranslate these pronouns to protect the doctrine of the separate personhood of the Spirit.

---

[1] "Greek Grammar and the Personality of the Holy Spirit," Bulletin for Biblical Research 13.1 (2003) 122, Institute for Biblical Research, 2003.

Patrick Navas states, *"it is quite natural to refer to the Spirit as 'it,' just as we refer to the wind or human breath with the pronoun as neuter. In fact, the Greek word pnuema is, in terms of grammar, neuter in gender."*[2] When I have a due damage to my car accidently, I call it a "Fender Bender." When translators do not translate the proper gender for pronouns, I call this a "Gender Bender." Below is the word for word, English to the Greek translation of Romans 8:16.

ITSELF	THE	SPIRIT	BEARS WITNESS	THE	SPIRIT	OUR
αὐτὸ	τὸ	πνεῦμα	συμμαρτυρεῖ	τῷ	πνεύματι	ἡμῶν

The Greek word for 'itself' is *auto* is a neuter pronoun *not* a masculine pronoun. See below to compare how the Greek pronoun used in Romans 8:16 would have been *autos* instead of *auto* if the Spirit was to be referred to as himself instead of itself.

Singular	*3rd p. masc.*	*3rd p. fem.*	*3rd p. neut.*
Nominative	αὐτός	αὐτή	αὐτό
Genitive	αὐτοῦ	αὐτῆς	αὐτοῦ
Dative	αὐτῷ	αὐτῇ	αὐτῷ
Accusative	αὐτόν	αὐτήν	αὐτό

Using the neuter pronoun to define the Spirit is a solid, biblical reason to conclude that the Spirit is not its own individual.

---

[2] Navas, Patrick. Divine Truth or Human Tradition?: A Reconsideration of the Orthodox Doctrine of the Trinity in Light of the Hebrew and Christian Scriptures . AuthorHouse. Kindle Edition.

Chapter Fifty

SPIRIT PRONOUNS

The New Testament does exclusively use neuter pronouns in reference to the Spirit, though there are a few instances where the Holy Spirit seems to be given a masculine pronoun. Dr. Daniel Wallace is a Biblical Greek scholar and professor at Dallas Theological Seminary. He is the cream of the crop of Greek scholars and a highly respected conservative Christian.

Daniel Wallace stresses that when the Spirit seemingly is assigned a masculine pronoun, these instances refer to the *paraclete*, not the Holy Spirit. The Greek grammar points back to the Advocate or Helper as the "he and whom," not the Holy Spirit.

"But when the <u>Helper</u>(*Advocate or Greek paraclete)* **comes, whom**(*correctly translated as masculine pronoun)* **I will send to you from the Father, the Spirit of truth, who**(*actually is a neuter pronoun and should be translated 'which')* **proceeds from the Father, <u>he</u> will bear witness about me.**
(John 15:26 ESV)

Most translations assume the pronoun 'he' refers to the Spirit of truth but actually refers to the person of the Advocate.

When we are in a courtroom, we need an Advocate to stand with us and beside us to bear witness for us. When we pray to the Father, Jesus stands beside us, defending us. In the

Old Testament, when an Israelite brought a sacrifice, the priest did not inspect the one bringing the offering. Only the offering was inspected, and once determined an acceptable sacrifice, the sins of the worshipper were covered. When we come to the Judge of the universe, we stand with our sacrifice and Advocate, the Lord Jesus, and our sins are forgiven. The Father is not looking at us when He forgives us– He is looking at our Advocate Christ Jesus.

The word *paraclete* means to *"call to one's side"* and is known as *"one who consoles, one who intercedes on our behalf, a comforter or an advocate."*[3] Jesus is our *paraclete*:

> **But if anybody does sin, we have one who speaks to the Father in our defense(*paraclete*)– Jesus Christ, the Righteous One.** (1 John 2:1 ESV)

John says that Jesus is the "Paraclete" in 1 John 2:1. But the Spirit is described as another "Paraclete" in John 14:16. The renowned Catholic scholar Raymond Brown believes that the Spirit is understood to be the ascended Christ. He writes that *"in the gospel of John, Jesus would have been a Paraclete in his earthly ministry, while in 1 John, Jesus is a Paraclete in heaven before the Father."*[4] Raymond Brown is referring to John 14:16, where Jesus says, **"And I will ask the Father, and he will give you another Helper**(*Greek paraclete*), **to be with you forever** (ESV)." Jesus

---

[3] Zodhiates, Spiros, and John R. Kohlenberger. *The Hebrew-Greek Key Study Bible: New International Version.* Chattanooga, TN: AMG Pub., 1996. 1659.
[4] Brown, Raymond, Doubleday, The Epistles of John

says He will send another but then tells his disciples that He will come to them.

But the Advocate(*Greek word: paraclete),* **the Holy Spirit, which the Father will send in my name, that one will teach you all things, and will remind you of all that I said to you. You heard how I told you, 'I go away, and I come to you.'**

(John 14:26,28 TNT)

Jesus repeats his words from 10 verses earlier that He would be with us. Here on earth, Jesus is with us, but no longer in His physical body. He is with us through His Spirit, and we are not left alone without guidance, protection, and care. **"I will not leave you as orphans; I will come to you"** (John 14:18 ESV).

The Paraclete is called the Holy Spirit in John 14:26 and then called Jesus Christ, the Righteous One in 1 John 2:1. The Gospel of John and 1 John are written by the same author. Someone said that the difference between Jesus and the Holy Spirit could not be separated by the sharpest razor. I believe the Spirit is the person of Jesus or the person of the Father. The Spirit does not have its own personhood but is the very presence of the Father or the Son.

Church fathers introduced the Trinity as the mystery of how our God exists. The mysterious part, however, is not the Trinity but instead how His Spirit works among His people. His Spirit is breathed into us to transform us into His divine image. The most basic understanding of the Spirit is moving air. Our God will sometimes move like a breath and sometimes like a hurricane. We cannot control how His Spirit will come!

Chapter Fifty-One

POWER TO CHANGE

The Greek language allows the authors to change the pronouns when necessary. The Greek language uses masculine(he, him), feminine(she, her), and neuter(it, that) to assist the reader in determining what actions are connected to which nouns. Modern translators have taken the liberty to change the gender of the pronouns when translating. As a translator, I understand that the general rule is that only the original author has the right to change the gender of the pronoun.

There are some examples of Biblical authors who changed the gender of a pronoun to help clarify their point. Paul uses the grammatically feminine word "head" for Christ in Colossians 2:19.[5] Yet when he uses a pronoun to refer back to the word "head," he chooses a masculine pronoun.

Holding fast to the Head(feminine), **from whom**(masculine) **the whole body, nourished and knit together.**

The whom is Christ. The apostle Paul broke the rules of grammar to communicate appropriately that Christ, as the head is a "he" and not a "she." The original authors can change the gender of pronouns as needed for clarification purposes. But

---

[5] https://restitutio.org/2015/11/05/translating-the-holy-spirit/

148

translators should not change pronouns to advance their theology. Here is another example of Matthew changing the gender of a pronoun for clarification purposes.

Before him will be gathered all the nations(neuter), and he will separate them(masculine) one from another as a shepherd separates the sheep from the goats.

(Matthew 25:32 ESV)

The Greek word for the nations is neuter, but Matthew refers to them using the masculine αὐτοὺς (them) rather than the neuter αὐτά (them). He does so because "the nations" are groups of people, not things, and it sounds more natural to refer to nations as masculine rather than neuter.[6]

If the New Testament writers could bend gender from impersonal to personal when neuter words referred to persons, then we should expect the same protocol when referring to the Spirit—if the authors of the New Testament really believed the Spirit was a separate person.

Not once have I heard someone refer to Jesus as "it," but I will often listen to how people refer to the Spirit. Even those most thoroughly convinced that the Spirit is a separate person of the Godhead often "accidentally" refer to the Spirit as "it" in casual conversation. Is this a Freudian slip?

"RECEIVE THE HOLY SPIRIT" – JESUS

---

[6] https://restitutio.org/2015/11/05/translating-the-holy-spirit/

Chapter Fifty-Two

PRONOUN SWAP

We cannot metaphorically throw all "pronoun adjusters" involved in Bible translation under the bus at this point. I am referring to those who have changed the gender of the pronoun for the spirit from "it" to "he." English does not usually use masculine or feminine pronouns to describe things. One might say of a car, "She is a beauty!" The Greek language has masculine, feminine, and neuter nouns, and pronouns, making translations challenging. Luke 5:37 describes the wine, which is a masculine noun, using a masculine pronoun(αὐτοὺς: see chart on page 140). Translators are wise to translate the pronoun as "it" and not "he."

And no one puts new wine into old wineskins. If he does, the new wine will burst the skins and it (αὐτοὺς) will be spilled and the skins will be destroyed. (Luke 5:37 ESV)

The Greek word *autos* is used for the pronoun describing wine, which is a masculine noun. Greek grammar rules will typically use a masculine pronoun when identifying masculine nouns. Yet to describe the new wine bursting and saying "he will be spilled" would not make sense in the translation. Therefore, translators changed the original pronoun from masculine to neuter to clarify the translation in this instance. Does this open the door for translators to pick and choose how to translate pronouns based on their theological preference?

In Mirror Study Bible, the translator uses the pronoun "she" for the Spirit instead of following the Greek.

But when she is come, the Spirit of truth, she will take you by the hand and guide you into the path of all truth. She will not draw attention to herself but will communicate and unveil everything she hears and discerns. (John 16:13 MSB).

If we allow translators in the most respected versions of the Bible to alter the Greek pronoun, who is to say the Mirror Study Bible is inaccurate? Though I'm afraid I have to disagree with this translation, I do not fault the translator any worse than modern translators who used masculine pronouns to define the Spirit. The John 16:31 text is now stretched to include a feminine side of our God.[7] I do not think this was the intention of Apostle John. If it were, John would have changed the pronoun for the Spirit to a feminine pronoun αὕτη (See chart on page 142).

When there is a doubt, follow the literal translation using the neuter pronouns(itself, it, which) when referring to the Spirit. We have looked at three examples of translators using all three pronouns "he, she, it" to define the Spirit. If the original authors of these words wanted to emphasize the Spirit as a "he" or "she," they had the power to communicate it if they desired. Yet no

---

[7] To justify his position on John 16:13, Francois du Toit, translator of the Mirror Study Bible, says, "While spirit is in the neuter gender, truth is feminine. In Hebrew, the word for spirit is רוּחַ ruach which is Feminine." du Toit, Francois. Mirror Study Bible . Kindle Edition.

author of any New Testament writings ever changed the gender of the pronoun describing the Spirit. I believe that fact is noteworthy.

THE HOLY SPIRIT WAS GIVEN TO US SO THAT WE COULD BE LIKE JESUS. OUR GOD MADE US IN HIS IMAGE SO THAT WE CARRY WITHIN US HIS SPIRIT. HE DID NOT MAKE US DIFFERENTLY, POTENTIALLY HINDERING OUR RELATIONSHIP. HE MADE US LIKE HIM, SO THAT WE CAN RELATE TO HIM. I AM SO GLAD THAT MY CHILDREN ARE MADE IN MY IMAGE. IMAGINE IF THEY WERE BORN A DIFFERENT SPECIES? A SIMPLE HUG OR INTERACTION, WHICH IS THE ESSENCE OF LIFE, WOULD BECOME DIFFICULT! IN THE SAME WAY, GOD HAS MADE US LIKE HIM, FOR THE VERY PURPOSE OF RELATIONSHIP. AND JUST LIKE JESUS, WE CAN BE A VESSEL OF HIS SPIRIT ALSO! THAT IS WHY PAUL TELLS US THAT THE HOPE OF GLORY IS "CHRIST IN YOU!" THE HOLY SPIRIT CONNECTS US TO GOD THE FATHER AND THE LORD JESUS CHRIST IN SUCH A WAY THAT HIS PRESENCE IS FELT, AND EXPERIENCED.

Chapter Fifty-Three

NO THIRD PERSON

When the apostle Paul describes the Spirit, he refers to it belonging to our God in the same manner that every man has a spirit. We are created in the image of our God. Paul says we cannot know the deep things of our God unless we experience his Spirit.

For who among men knows the things of a man, except the spirit of the man, which(*neuter pronoun*) is in him? Even so, no one knows the things of our God, except the Spirit of our God. (1 Corinthians 2:11 TNT)

Paul refers to the spirit of the man in him using the neuter article τò to be translated as "which." The same neuter article is used to declare the Spirit from our God. Many translations change the article to a masculine pronoun and translate this verse as the "Spirit who is from God."

But we received, not the spirit of the world, but the Spirit which(*neuter pronoun*) is from our God, that we might know the things that were freely given to us by our God. (1 Corinthians 2:12 TNT)

Dr. Wallace affirms that "...*there is no text in the NT that clearly or even probably affirms the personality of the Holy Spirit through the*

153

route of Greek grammar."[8] I would clarify that no text clarifies or affirms a separate personality of the Spirit– the personality of the Spirit is either the Father or the Son.

I believe we should not oppose the personhood of the Spirit but instead should see the Spirit as the person of Father or the Son. Neuter articles identify the Spirit as belonging to the Father or the Son.

Dr. Wallace writes that the Greek New Testament does not offer any textual evidence that the Spirit is its own person. The exclusive use of neuter pronouns when defining the Spirit should lead us to conclude that the person of the Spirit is the person of the Father or the Son. He writes:

If the NT authors indeed conceived of the Holy Spirit as a person, we may well expect to see natural gender taking precedent over grammatical gender in various passages that speak of the Spirit.[9]

Dr. Wallace says that the Greek authors would have changed the pronouns in the original language. The Spirit would have been given masculine pronouns (i.e., He, who, whom) instead of neuter pronouns (i.e., it, that, which).

THE SPIRIT OF GOD IS NOT ANOTHER PERSON FOR US TO FOCUS ON; WE MUST SEEK AFTER THE FATHER AND THE SON.

---

[8] "Greek Grammar and the Personality of the Holy Spirit," Bulletin for Biblical Research 13.1 (2003) 122, Institute for Biblical Research, 2003.
[9] Ibid, 99

Chapter Fifty-Four

RULES OF GRAMMAR

As I was translating the Name Translation Bible, I recognized that I do not have the authority to change the pronoun from a neuter form to a masculine form, regardless of my theological preferences. Every reader of any Bible translation ought to be presented with the most accurate text possible. Once the text is in their hand, they can now determine their theology.

Most theologians believe the Bible clearly defines the Holy Spirit as a separate person other than the Father and the Son. Daniel Wallace himself is a Trinitarian. But as a scholar and one who submits to the rules of grammar, Dr. Wallace summarizes his thoughts:

In sum, I have sought to demonstrate in this paper that the grammatical basis for the Holy Spirit's personality is lacking in the NT, yet this is frequently, if not usually, the first line of defense of that doctrine by many evangelical writers. But if grammar cannot legitimately be used to support the Spirit's personality, then perhaps we need to reexamine the rest of our basis for this theological commitment. I am not denying the doctrine of the Trinity, of course, but I am arguing that we need to ground our beliefs on a more solid foundation.[10]

[10] Ibid, 125

Wallace clearly articulates the absence of evidence in the grammar of the New Testament defending a third person in the Trinity. Wallace is not denying the Trinity, but he is questioning the interpretation of the existence of a third person of God based on the pronouns ascribed to the Spirit.

The challenge for theologians is the lack of clear evidence of the modern-day definition of the Trinity in the Bible. Early church fathers talked about the triad of the Father, Son, and the Spirit, but only later was the Trinity defined in terms of three persons, each being God. All Christians agree there is a Father, Son, and Holy Spirit, but many question how they relate, exist, and interact.

The theology for the separate personhood of the Holy Spirit relies almost exclusively in the writings of John. We find the masculine pronouns used in the gospel of John when referring to the Advocate(*paraclete* in Greek). No doubt this is why many can embrace the Spirit as a separate person, though I believe the Advocate is pointing to the risen Christ. But notice that the same author of the gospel of John writes in 1 John.

We proclaim to you what we have seen and heard so that you also may have fellowship with us. And our fellowship is with the Father and with his Son, Jesus Christ. (1 John 1:3 NIV)
We fellowship with the Father and the Son according to 1 John 1:3, not the Father, Son, and Spirit. As the Spirit is not included as a separate person, the Trinity falls apart, and a clearer understanding of the two powers in Heaven is revealed.

Chapter Fifty-Five

JOHN OR PAUL?

John lay at the bosom of Jesus. He was a feeler. John wrote from the gut, colored outside the lines, and was not the intellectual as Paul was. The writings of John are not less weighty than that of Paul, but instead, note the differences in style. Our God used both of these men for a purpose and to have their writings today in the New Testament is a true gift.

John wrote more of the New Testament than anyone else, except for Paul. The difference between Paul and John is evident in their writings. When we balance John's artistic style with Paul's straightforward writing style, our understanding of how the Holy Spirit interacts with the Father and Son may change. In his writings, Paul is highly intellectual, rational, and forceful, whereas John is more artistic, creative, and imaginative. Paul wrote a thesis, but John painted a picture. Most theologians pull heavily from the writings of John to get their understanding of the Spirit. John was a poetic writer who used lots of imagery and creativity. You can sense the difference dramatically when you read Paul's style in comparison.

Paul wrote in a direct manner, unlike John. Paul dealt with issues as an apostle with great passion and intellect. He did not write as mystically as John did. We should not read John in the same manner that we read Paul. John wrote down vast

157

amounts of mystical revelation and visions that he had experienced, while Paul wrote more to groups of believers who needed correction and direction. John wrote from a heavenly perspective, while Paul wrote from more of an earthly perspective.

The Gospel of John and 1 John were written by the same author, yet most of our theology for the Holy Spirit as a separate person comes from John's gospel. Yet a slow read through 1 John might surprise you about John's theology. He makes clear the importance of the Father and the Son, but fails to mention the Spirit: **"No one who denies the Son has the Father. Whoever confesses the Son has the Father also"** (1 John 2:23 ESV).

The Apostle Paul wrote to the Philippians that he was grateful for the **"...help of the Spirit of Jesus Christ"** (Philippians 1:19 ESV). Paul writes to the Roman Church, **"...if anyone does not have the Spirit of Christ he does not belong to Christ"** (Romans 8:9). Galatians 4:6 says, **"Our God sent the Spirit of His Son into our hearts, crying out, "Abba, Father!""** (Galatians 4:6 TNT).

Luke writes in the book of Acts about Paul and his team not being able to cross a border because **"...the Spirit of Jesus would not allow them to"** (Acts 16:7). Why would Luke write about the Spirit of Jesus and not just say the Holy Spirit? The most logical conclusion, in my opinion, is to identify the Holy Spirit as the Spirit of Jesus and the Father. Whatever spirit they breathe is holy.

158

Breath is what makes a person come alive as a living being. Your breath or spirit is what makes you alive, but it is not another person outside of you. The breath of our God is what makes us come alive. The Holy Spirit is the mysterious way we enter His nature and being. Embrace the sacred Spirit that both the Father and Son give us to live an empowered life in His nature.

WHEN THE LORD HIMSELF WALKED THIS EARTH, HE MODELED HOW WE SHOULD INTERACT WITH THE FATHER AND HOW WE SHOULD MINISTER. FROM THE VERY BEGINNING OF THE MINISTRY OF JESUS, "...THE HOLY SPIRIT DESCENDED ON HIM IN BODILY FORM LIKE A DOVE." (LUKE 3:22) REMEMBER, THE SPIRIT WAS HERE ON THE EARTH WHILE JESUS WAS MINISTERING. THE HOLY SPIRIT IS THE SPIRIT OF GOD, THE SPIRIT OF CHRIST, OR THE SPIRIT. WE HAVE IN OUR MINDS THAT THERE IS A PERSON CALLED "HOLY SPIRIT" INSTEAD OF SEEING THE SPIRIT AS THE POWER, THE LOVE, AND THE CONNECTING FORCE OF THE KINGDOM OF GOD.

Chapter Fifty-Six

THREE'S A CROWD

The saying, "Two's Company, Three's a Crowd," means one person is usually ignored when three are present. The statement also infers a lack of intimacy when more than two come together. Of course, we do not shape our theology based on cultural statements, but this idea has a practical side. Practicing Trinitarians tend to forget someone– and that person is often Jesus. You can say "Amen" or "Ouch!"

The Trinity creates the most significant resistance when evangelizing people of other beliefs. When I am witnessing to a Jehovah's Witness(JW), I will always bring the conversation back to the place of their perspective on Jesus. But most JW's attack the Trinity because it is one of the most complex doctrines to defend. They do not worship Jesus. They do not honor Jesus the same way they honor Jehovah(Yahweh).

This section will provide you with the history and reasons the doctrine of the Trinity has been embraced by the large majority of Bible believers. I have spent over ten thousand hours on this topic to understand the heart behind this well-respected doctrine better.

Note that there is not just one definition of the Trinity. Many of the early church fathers used the word Trinity but not necessarily as defined as our current definition. The most basic understanding of the word Trinity is the Father, Son, and Holy Spirit– three separate persons, all of the same God substance, co-eternal and co-equal.

So, when asked if I believe in the Trinity, I like to clarify that I believe in the Father, Son, and the Holy Spirit. The relationship between the three of this triad is where I differ.

The word Trinity was not mentioned in the writings of early church fathers until about 150 years after the resurrection of Jesus. A few Scriptures connect the Father, Son, and Holy Spirit in one sentence, but more often, the emphasis is on the Father and the Son. John, the apostle, repeatedly points to the Father and Son relationship in his letters.

This is the antichrist, he who denies the Father and the Son. No one who denies the Son has the Father. Whoever confesses the Son has the Father also.

(1 John 2:23 ESV)

John writes that the spirit of the antichrist denies the Father and the Son. If the triune concept of God is central to the faith of the first disciples, why was the Spirit omitted? Instead, the apostle John affirms there is opposition to the two powers in heaven.

The mysterious part of this triad is not the Father and the Son but instead the Spirit. Once the Spirit was introduced as another separate person, confusion instead of clarity ensued.

Chapter Fifty-Seven

FORGOTTEN GOD

One error common in the body of Christ is to emphasize Holy Spirit more than Jesus. I think this is a mistake, and Christianity should be Christ-centered. Jesus should be our best friend. The Holy Spirit is part of our God-experience– connecting us with the Father, Son, and each other. The life and Spirit of our God and His Son fills us and grants us the divine nature.

When we introduce the Holy Spirit as another person, Jesus tends to be forgotten. We are trying to get to the Father by the Spirit instead of through Jesus.

Imagine you walk into a restaurant and sit in a booth with three other people facing you. You address them all as "God." In fear of ignoring one of them, you begin to speak over their heads, trusting you are doing the right thing. As you talk to "God," sometimes you say Father, other times you say Jesus, and other times you say Holy Spirit.

Where confusion exists, hesitation and doubt occur. Great minds that have done extensive studies on the Trinity, such as Saint Augustine and Thomas Aquinas, arrive at this basic conclusion:

The Trinity:
Try to Understand It and
You'll Lose Your Mind.

162

Try to Deny It and
You'll LOSE YOUR SOUL!

The concept of the Trinity or the triad of the Father, Son, and Holy Spirit was first conceived around 180 AD by the theologian Origen. It soon gained popularity throughout the Greek-speaking world and eventually became the enforced doctrine of the Roman Empire under Theodosius in 381 A.D.[11] Many scholars believe that this year signified the closing of the Western mind and made it a criminal act to think differently. The mind of an individual was forced to accept concepts that could not be understood. Coercion and threats, and acts of violence were placed upon individuals who questioned ideas outside those deemed orthodox.

The concept of the triune God is shrouded in mystery and has become a stumbling block for many. The greatest theologians of all church history– Augustine and Thomas Aquinas– wrote large treatises on the subject only to conclude that it is beyond understanding.[12] The attractive aspect of the Trinity is that it must be accepted by faith. The concept is added

---

[11] In his Theological Orations, delivered in Constantinople in 380, he drew on a tradition… that ultimately the nature of God is a mystery and that the proper response to questions about his nature should be silence.
Freeman, Charles. The Closing of the Western Mind: The Rise of Faith and the Fall of Reason . Knopf Doubleday Publishing Group. Kindle Edition.
[12] Thomas Aquinas quotes Augustine. "But, as Augustine says: 'When we say there are three who bear witness in heaven, the Father, the Word, and the Holy Ghost, and it is asked, Three what? the answer is, Three persons." Therefore, person signifies essence.' *Aquinas, Thomas. Summa Theologica (Complete & Unabridged) (p. 149). Coyote Canyon Press. Kindle Edition.*

to the other mysteries of the faith and boldly defended by most orthodox theologians.

The concept of the Trinity was introduced to Christian theology to attempt to solve the monotheistic problem that Jesus created. The Trinity seemingly creates more problems than it solves, yet Christians are expected to accept it as a mystery or be deemed a heretic.

CONFUSION WILL ONLY DRIVE AWAY JEWS AND MUSLIMS FROM THE TRUTH. THE WORDS, "GODHEAD, DIVINITY AND TRINITY," HINDER THE REAL MESSAGE OF THE KINGDOM. IF OUR CORE DOCTRINE IS UNCLEAR, WE WILL LOSE SOULS FOR ETERNITY AND WE WILL BE HELD ACCOUNTABLE FOR OUR TEACHINGS. THERE IS A STORY ABOUT A MUSLIM EVANGELIST IN AFRICA WHO REACHED A CERTAIN VILLAGE IN ORDER TO SPREAD ISLAM. HE ASKED ONE OF THE LOCALS, 'DO YOU PREFER TO WORSHIP ONE GOD AND HAVE FOUR WIVES, OR TO WORSHIP THREE GODS AND HAVE ONE WIFE?' THE AFRICAN SAID, 'I LIKE FOUR WOMEN, AND I DON'T CARE WHICH GOD. I WANT FOUR WOMEN.'

Chapter Fifty-Eight

REAL ORTHODOXY

Orthodoxy is defined as right or correcting thinking. Ortho means "straight or right" and doxy means "words." Theologians try to define what set of beliefs brings a person to the place of salvation. Many churches adopt creeds, which consist of concise statements that must be confessed, authorizing a person to be saved. Salvation is activated through a belief and a confession. Paul wrote in this letter to the church in Rome:

If you confess with your mouth that Jesus is Lord and believe in your heart that God raised him from the dead, you will be saved. For with the heart, one believes and is justified, and with the mouth one confesses and is saved.

(Romans 10:9-10 ESV).

Our salvation is activated by faith, not by works. We are saved by confessing that "Jesus is Lord" and believing that our God has raised this Jesus from the grave. Our God did raise Jesus from the dead, and by confessing Jesus as Lord, our salvation is granted. Paul writes to the Philippians:

Therefore, God has highly exalted him and bestowed on him the name that is above every name, so that at the name of Jesus every knee should bow, in heaven and on earth and under the earth, and every tongue confess that Jesus Christ is Lord, to the glory of God the Father.

165

(Philippians 2:9-11 ESV)

Honoring Jesus as King just as Yahweh is honored as King is key to having a saving theology. There is a requirement to believe something particular for righteousness to occur. Honor the Son in the same way one honors the Father is key.

That all may honor the Son just as they honor the Father. He who does not honor the Son does not honor the Father, who sent him. (John 5:22-23 NIV)

In theological terms, orthodoxy is based upon the person of Jesus Christ. In simple terms, we must treat Him in the same way we treat the Father. But we should treat them as two separate persons.

Now I want you to realize that the head of every man is Christ, and the head of the woman is man, and the head of Christ is God. (1 Corinthians 11:3 NIV).

Paul writes clearly that the head of Christ is God. I like to use the analogy of president Bush senior and President Bush junior. Both were presidents and ruled in that office during different eras. From the perspective of an American citizen, we treat the father and the son with the same respect as the office requires. But the son recognizes he came from the father, and from his perspective, the father is greater, as Jesus says in John 14:28, **"...for the Father is greater than I."** The early creeds tried too hard to see our God as one entity and therefore created a theological doctrine that accommodated their intentions.

Chapter Fifty-Nine

CAUSE OF HERESY

I think the "Safety First" idea could be applied to the Trinity. This doctrine guarantees that Jesus will be treated with the same honor and respect as is due his Father. Jesus is to be worshipped as the One who sits at the right hand of the Father. The source or head of Christ is God Himself.

I have concluded that orthodoxy is not exclusively Trinitarian. Honoring Jesus as one honors the Father is orthodoxy. I am very wary of assuming that orthodoxy should be based on the notion of a triune Godhead– an idea that was not even discussed or written about until over a century and a half after Jesus' resurrection.

Let's say you had a disease called heresy. You went to the drugstore, and you had a few options, but all of the options also had a few side effects. The most common way of dealing with heresy is a medication called Trinity. It works quite well and historically has been on the market the longest with a solid record of keeping heresy out of one's system. The side effects are listed as confusion, disorientation, and hard to swallow. It is not recommended for outsiders. But it does kill heresy.

I have sought to define heresy as an improper view of Christ. My summary is the way you avoid heresy is you treat Jesus the same way you treat the Father. Though Jesus submitted to His Father, He holds the position of King of kings to the world. As a Son, He is fully obedient to the Father. As our Lord and Savior, He must be treated with the same honor as the Father.

The Trinity secures the most important doctrine: Jesus is honored in the same way the Father is honored. Theologians use the term "Christology" to define a person's view of Jesus. The Trinity secures a high Christology. I believe this doctrine has prevailed and stood the test of time because of its ability to secure the beauty of responding to Jesus as one would the Father.

There is a danger when Jesus loses His place in the hearts of believers. Arius, a bishop of the early church, taught that "There was a time when the Son was not!" He would emphasize the concept of Jesus being created, and this idea was rejected by most of the early church fathers. Arius set into motion ideas that inferred Jesus was not everything His Father was. The doctrine of the Trinity was solidified into church doctrine as a reaction to his teachings.

Cults do not give Jesus His proper place in their worship. The Trinitarian belief is one model that allows for Jesus to maintain his proper position in the hearts and minds of its adherents. I believe our minds embrace the 'three in one' model of a God for this reason. Our hearts then embrace the Trinity as a sort of mystery– fully accepting though not fully understood. In a way, this is quite Biblical to embrace with our hearts that which we cannot understand with our minds. But I disagree

168

with the conclusion that the Trinity is the best Biblical model of understanding the relationship between the Father, Son, and the Holy Spirit. Accepting that there are two powers in heaven stretches the concept of monotheism but lands well in the Biblical narrative.

I CANNOT TELL PEOPLE TO MERELY BELIEVE IN GOD. PEOPLE OF MANY DIVERSE FAITHS BELIEVE IN GOD. BUT JAMES, 2:19 SAYS, "YOU BELIEVE THAT THERE IS ONE GOD. GOOD! EVEN THE DEMONS BELIEVE THAT— AND SHUDDER." THE CONFESSION THAT BRINGS SALVATION IS THE ACKNOWLEDGEMENT OF GOD'S SON JESUS CHRIST. ROMANS 10:9 SAYS, "IF YOU CONFESS WITH YOUR MOUTH JESUS IS LORD, AND BELIEVE IN YOUR HEART THAT GOD RAISED HIM FROM THE DEAD, YOU WILL BE SAVED." I BELIEVE THAT OUR EMPHASIS IN EVANGELISM AND TEACHING MUST BE THAT JESUS IS LORD, THE SON OF GOD WHO IS ENTHRONED AS THE NEW KING.

Chapter Sixty

GOD SUBSTANCE?

With the influence of Greek thought, philosophers began introducing statements into religious discussions like "the deity of Christ," "the substance of God," and "the Trinity." These concepts begin the conversation about our God with the question, "What is God made of?" and "Is Jesus made in the exact substance as the Father?" When unbiblical language and ideas are used to explain the Bible, we often drift into a place of spiritual confusion.[13] Early church fathers resisted the

---

[13] Athanasius had come to the conclusion that many opposed the Nicene Creed because they feared that the assertion that the Son was of the same substance as the Father could be understood as meaning that there is no distinction between the Father and the Son. Therefore, some preferred not to say "of the same substance," but rather "of a similar substance." The two Greek words were homoousios (of the same substance) and *homoiousios* (of a similar substance). The Council of Nicaea had declared the Son to be *homoousios* with the Father. But now many were saying that they would rather affirm that the Son was *homoiousios* with the Father. At an earlier time, Athanasius had insisted on the Nicene formula declaring that those who said "of a similar substance" were as heretical as the Arians. But now the elderly bishop of Alexandria was ready to see the legitimate concern of those Christians who, while refusing Arianism, were not ready to give up the distinction between the Father and the Son. Through a series of negotiations, Athanasius convinced many of these Christians that the formula of Nicaea could be interpreted in such a way as to respond to the concerns of those who would rather say, "of a similar substance." Finally, in a synod gathered in Alexandria in A.D. 362, Athanasius and his followers declared that it was acceptable to refer to the Father, Son, and Holy Spirit as "one substance" as long as this was not understood as obliterating the distinction among the three, and that it was also legitimate to speak of "three substances" as long as this was not understood as if there were three gods. On the basis of this understanding, of the church rallied in its support to the Council of Nicaea, whose doctrine was eventually ratified at the Second Ecumenical Council, gathered in Constantinople in A.D. 381. But Athanasius would

philosophical language being used in the creeds that were written at the Council of Nicaea.[14] Later accounts of this council in 325 A.D describe an intense spiritual battle.[15]

CONSTANTINE WAS THE FIRST CHRISTIAN EMPEROR OF ROMAN EMPIRE, AND HE PRESIDED OVER THE COUNCIL OF NICAEA, THE FIRST OF SEVEN COUNCILS. MANY SCHOLARS CONSIDER CONSTANTINE'S CONVERSION THE MOST SIGNIFICANT EVENT IN HUMAN HISTORY.[16] HE WAS A VERY INFLUENTIAL AND SUCCESSFUL EMPEROR. HOWEVER, CONSTANTINE INVOLVED HIMSELF IN RELIGIOUS MATTERS AND CONTROLLED THE OUTCOMES OF THESE COUNCILS.

---

not live to see the final victory of the cause to which he devoted most of his life. Gonzalez, Justo L. (2010-07-25). Story of Christianity: Volume 1: The Early Church to the Reformation (Kindle Locations 3738-3740). Harper Collins, Inc.. Kindle Edition.

[14] But the term 'essence' has been taken up by the Fathers rather unwisely, and gives offense because it is not understood by the people. It is also not contained in the Scriptures. For these reasons we have decided to do away with it, and that no use at all shall be made of it or in the future in connection with God, because the divine Scriptures nowhere use it of the Father and the Son. But we say that the Son is like the Father in all things, as the Holy Scriptures say and teach.14 (Soc. H.E. ii 37; Ath. De syn.8)

[15] The situation was very confused. The debates, it was said a century later, resembled a battle in the dark, no one knowing whether he was striking at friend or foe.'" Frend, William, H.C. The Early Church (p. 140). Kindle Edition.

[16] Carroll, James. *Constantine's Sword: the Church and the Jews : a History*. Boston: Houghton Mifflin, 2001. 171

Chapter Sixty-One

RELATION EMPHASIS

My journey has compelled me to define a model other than the Trinity, with the relational emphasis that is obvious to all who read. This Biblical model emphasizes not Three in One, but a Father and Son Dynasty, where the Son rules the kingdom, seated on His Father's throne. Jesus and the Father are the two powers in heaven.

Most scholars will tell you the word "Trinity" came about around 150 years after the time of Christ. The phrase "The Father, The Son and The Holy Spirit" are found in the writings at least as early as the 2nd generation of the disciples, if not earlier. The Trinity can only be inferred as Biblical because it is not implicitly described in the Bible. Jesus never used the word Trinity nor did any other Biblical author.

Christians became quite divided over the use of unbiblical words and concepts. Councils were established to bring clarity to the beliefs of Christians. By the 4th Century of Christianity, the dividing lines had been drawn between Trinitarians and Non-Trinitarians. Ultimately, the Trinitarians won. But in the process of this victory, much bloodshed and violence occurred.

As the church won favor with the Roman Empire in the 4th Century, even the government itself became involved in the conflict. Soon, the sword would be used to enforce doctrinal beliefs, and the blood of many followers of Christ still cries out from the ground. The Roman Emperor Constantine issued a decree in 333 A.D. in hopes of bringing unity to the body of Christ. He condemns the writings of Arius, a bishop of Christianity, and declares the death penalty for anyone found with any of his writings.[17]

Christians became quite divided over the use of unbiblical words and concepts. Councils were established to bring clarity to the beliefs of Christians. By the 4th Century of Christianity, the dividing lines had been drawn between Trinitarians and Non-Trinitarians. Ultimately, the Trinitarians won. But in the process of this victory, much bloodshed and violence occurred.

Regardless of your stance on the Trinity, please, take a moment and repent for the sins of division, hatred, and murder in the church. Disagreement over doctrinal issues should have never resulted in the killing of other human beings. Whatever position you decide to accept or doctrine you decide to embrace, this must be done with a heart of humility, compassion, and

---

[17] If any treatise composed by Arius should be discovered, let it be consigned to the flames, in order that no memorial of him may be by any means left. This therefore I [Constantine] decree, that if anyone shall be detected in concealing a book compiled by Arius, and shall not instantly bring it forward and burn it, the penalty for this offence shall be death; for immediately after conviction the criminal shall suffer capital punishment."

love.[18] The church has some embarrassing history that we can take to the cross of Jesus. Pray this prayer of forgiveness below:

FATHER, I COME IN THE NAME OF JESUS. I ACKNOWLEDGE AND REPENT OF THE DIVISION, BLOODSHED, AND VIOLENCE THAT HAS OCCURRED IN THE BODY OF CHRIST THROUGHOUT HISTORY. I PLACE THIS GENERATIONAL INIQUITY ON THE CROSS OF CHRIST AND DECLARE IT FORGIVEN OVER MY LIFE AND ALL FUTURE GENERATIONS. I ASK FOR CLEAN HANDS AND A PURE HEART AS I CONSIDER THE BELIEF SYSTEM PASSED ON TO ME FROM MY FOREFATHERS. FILL ME WITH YOUR HOLY SPIRIT AS I READ YOUR WORD. IN JESUS' NAME, AMEN!

---

[18] Paul wrote, **"If I ...do not have love, I am only a resounding gong or a clanging cymbal"** (1 Corinthians 13:1).

Chapter Sixty-Two

ONE MEDIATOR ONLY

The Trinity establishes the position of Jesus in heaven, being everything His Father is. The Trinity includes and personifies the Spirit– mystifying instead of simplifying the concept of the person of the Father and the Son. Trinitarians have a high Christology which is necessary but at the cost of confusion concerning that which is simple.

When the concept of the Trinity became the doctrine of the Western church, the role of Jesus as a mediator became distorted. How could Jesus be a mediator between both man and God and also be the God of heaven? Paul clearly teaches that Jesus is between our God and men.

For there is one God and one mediator between God and men, the man Christ Jesus, who gave himself as a ransom for all men. (1 Timothy 2:5-6 NIV)

We know that the only saving source in the universe is the blood of Jesus Christ. He is the mediator between man and our God.

Jesus became so elevated and connected with the God of Heaven that we needed a more human mediator. That is why Mary worship and saints later developed into mediators, which is still the tradition of most Catholic churches. The force of the Trinitarian view led to this later deception which did not clearly separate the Father and Son into two distinct powers in heaven. This resulted in believers becoming unable to relate to Jesus any longer as a man. The Bible clearly celebrates the day when Jesus came in human flesh and became a man.

On a deep level of thought, the Trinity can make sense and, for some, even become something beautiful. But I do not believe this is the model the Bible gives us in how we are to approach the Father and the Son, nor does the Trinity accurately work in the Spirit. I always defaulted to the Trinitarian view because of the lack of an alternative.

The Trinity defines "God" as being one God existing coequally in three distinct persons and who share the same essence or substance. Basically, the three persons define who God is, and the one substance defines what God is. Below is the traditional understanding of how the Trinity works for most theologians.

Father, Son, Spirit = The Who
God = The What

The ultimate result is you can still have one God and also make room for Jesus and the Spirit. Philosophically, a brilliant solution, but theologically, a challenge, as if trying to fit a square peg into a round hole.

Chapter Sixty-Three

TINTED GLASSES

There is needed to present a clear explanation of what is the most Biblical way to present the relationship and function of the Father, Son, and Holy Spirit. My previous writing entitled, Heaven's Dynasty, explained how the kingdom is a dynasty passed on from Father to Son. The Son is Jesus, and the Father is Yahweh. My summary declares that everything the Father is, Jesus is. Going beyond the previous statement merely complicates simplicity.

My ideas are not being circulated to condemn the Trinity but to understand the reason this doctrine has stood the test of time. There is a need to go beyond the Trinity. Christianity is at a place in this hour of tremendous growth, and our message must be clear and concise. The Trinity secures a vital truth. You can hold on to this doctrine and be solid and safe in your salvation.

My goal is to convince you to hold on to this vital truth but also to be willing to let go of any unnecessary language. Theologians ought not to use words not in Bible to convey the truths of the Bible. The Bible's emphasis is on a dynasty, not on a Trinity. Jesus is established as King over heaven and earth in the New Testament. The Father releases all authority to His Son Jesus. Yahweh is not just a God of power but also a God of empowerment. I present to you a much simpler concept to enhance your understanding of Scripture.

Church history reminds us of the controversy that the view of the Trinity brought to Christendom.[19] What we see is often determined by the lenses which we are looking through.

NOTED CHURCH HISTORY SCHOLAR JUSTO L. GONZALEZ, SAID:

A PERSON WEARING TINTED GLASSES CAN AVOID THE CONCLUSION THAT THE ENTIRE WORLD IS TINTED ONLY BY BEING CONSCIOUS OF THE GLASSES THEMSELVES. LIKEWISE, IF WE ARE TO BREAK FREE FROM AN UNDUE WEIGHT OF TRADITION, WE MUST BEGIN BY UNDERSTANDING WHAT THAT TRADITION IS, HOW WE CAME TO BE WHERE WE ARE, AND HOW PARTICULAR ELEMENTS IN OUR PAST COLOR OUR VIEW OF THE PRESENT. IT IS THEN THAT WE ARE FREE TO CHOOSE WHICH ELEMENTS IN THE PAST—AND IN THE PRESENT—WE WISH TO REJECT, AND WHICH WE WILL AFFIRM.[20]

---

[19] Athanasius had come to the conclusion that many opposed the Nicene Creed because they feared that the assertion that the Son was of the same substance as the Father could be understood as meaning that there is no distinction between the Father and the Son. Therefore, some preferred not to say, "of the same substance," but rather "of a similar substance

[20] Gonzalez, Justo L. (2010-07-25). Story of Christianity: Volume 1: The Early Church to the Reformation (Kindle Locations 323-329). Harper Collins, Inc. Kindle Edition.

Chapter Sixty-Four

JESUS BE THE CENTER

Once upon a time, there was a beautiful statue that was set up in a kingdom to honor the King. This statue was a constant reminder and landmark in the city of the King and always pointed to a stable and righteous King who presided over the region. But one day, some evil men came to the city and began to attack this beautiful statue, damaging it and desecrating this icon that once looked proudly over the city. Once the evil men were caught and expelled from the city, a huge scaffolding was erected around the statue in hopes of restoring the statue. As the work began, people began to become enamored with the scaffolding that stood surrounding the statue. They began to discuss the need to elaborate on the scaffolding to make it look more attractive, and suddenly more effort was being put toward the scaffolding than the statue it was erected to protect and beautify.

This story reminds me of the doctrine of the Trinity. The beautiful statue it was meant to protect is the high Christology of Jesus. The relationship between the Father and the Son– the concept that there were two powers in heaven, one named Yahweh, who most often assumed the title as God, and the one who was called the Father and the other named Jesus, the Son of our God, and most often called Lord. Sadly, the Trinity was erected to stop the belief that Jesus was some created being and not the other power in heaven. This scaffolding became the central focus, and though the scaffolding was often repaired and kept in good condition, the statue for which it was erected crumbled away in time.

The wrong assumption about theology distracts us from following God with a clear conscience and being effective in communicating the message of salvation. We often forget how our paradigm of the Bible has been deeply influenced by the force of church tradition. We must be humble, prayerful, and studious.

Chapter Sixty-Five

JEWISH BARRIERS

Since the second century, barriers have been raised between Jewishness and Jesus. Though Israel was hardened to the message of Jesus due to their unbelief, barriers have been raised higher and higher through lies, misinterpretations of scripture, and persecution. For spiritual reasons, Satan has purposed to strengthen the barriers throughout history because he knows that the union of the Jews and Jesus will bring his defeat.

When Jesus was rejected by the majority of Jewish leadership in the 1st century, the two power in heaven theory was also abandoned. Jesus fit into this model so perfectly that many Jews were thoroughly convinced of His messianic claims. Theological emphasis on monotheism was strengthened, and followers of Jesus were labeled as polytheists and betrayers of Judaism.

But deception also flourished in the predominantly Gentile church and their relationship with the Jew. Even today, we face many barriers which must be pulled down to reach the Jewish people, barriers of reason, emotion, and tradition. We must consider the historical perspective behind these anti-Jesus barriers. How to restore the Jewish ear is my prayer for the lost sheep of Israel this entire chapter is based upon Luke 22:45-51.

In Gethsemane, the disciples were confronted by Jesus:

"Why are you sleeping?" he asked them. "Get up and pray so that you will not fall into temptation" (Luke 22:46 NIV). The disciples slept while their master cried out concerning the situation that would soon be upon them. "Exhausted from sorrow" (vs. 45), the disciples slept instead of preparing themselves with prayer to face the temptations that would occur that night. As the events unfolded, the disciples crumbled under pressure due to the weakness of their own flesh.

Like the sleeping disciples, the church has been prayerless and weak in dealing with those who reject the Messiah. Satan seeks every opportunity to divide the Jew and Jesus, and most often, he does it best through the followers of Jesus.

IF THERE IS ONE THING THAT CHRISTIANS KNOW ABOUT THEIR RELIGION, IT IS THAT IT IS NOT JUDAISM. IF THERE IS ONE THING THAT JEWS KNOW ABOUT THEIR RELIGION, IT IS THAT IT IS NOT CHRISTIANITY. —RABBI DANIEL BOYARIN

Chapter Sixty-Six

ELECTRIC FENCES

Throughout history, adherents to both Judaism and Christianity have yielded to demonic spirits and have persecuted each other. At different times, whichever faith controlled the seat of power obligated itself to oppress the other. Lies were circulated, degrading each other's faith, and fences were established between the two faiths; and due to the bloodshed, the fences were electrified.

Satan's goal was to paint Jesus and Jewishness as opposing forces, never able to be reconciled. Even though both Judaism and Christianity have settled on the doctrine of monotheism, the chasm between the Jewish understanding and the Christian understanding of monotheism is wide.

In Acts 21:28, for example, when Paul is in Jerusalem, we find some Jews spreading falsehood about him, saying: **"Men of Israel, help us! This is the man who teaches all men everywhere against our people and our law and this place."** This lie was circulated not only to smear Paul but to bring doubt upon the commitment of a Jewish believer to his roots. This commitment that a Gentile and Jewish believer must have to his roots is vital to accomplish an effective witness to the Jewish people. Without it, large numbers of Jews will never accept their Messiah.

This same lie is evident even today. One of today's leading scholars in Judaism, George W. E. Nicklesburg, writes about the gospel of Matthew. He states that this is the most Jewish of all gospels, as most scholars would agree. But Nickelsburg makes some startling statements concerning Matthew's view of Israel. He claims Matthew believes that:

Israel has been stripped of its status of God's people, and the church- largely the Gentile in its constituency- has been raised up to this position.[21]

His point is that if the most Jewish gospel eliminates the role of Israel in God's plan, how could the rest of the New Covenant scriptures say anything better? Another quote of Nickelsburg makes this presumption:

Moreover, he (Matthew) does not hope for restoration and reconstruction, nor does he presume at the very least the continued existence of the Jews as God's people[22].

To a Jew, to say his race is no longer special to the heart of God is to discredit the Hebrew Scriptures. How can this be true when God spoke to Abraham in Genesis 17:7:

I will establish my covenant as an everlasting covenant between me and you and your descendants after you for the generations to come, to be your God, and the God of your descendants after you

---

[21] George W. E. Nicklesburg, Jewish Literature Between the Bible and the Mishnah (Philadelphia, PA: Fortress Press, 1981), p.304
[22] Ibid, p.304

Chapter Sixty-Seven

NOURISHING SAP

The Middle East conflict between the Jew and the Muslim is over the very next verse speaking of, **"the...land of Canaan,"** (Genesis 17:8) and who it belongs to, yet Christianity has espoused to an even greater lie than that of the Muslims! Muslims claim to have rights to the land of Jew, yet some Christian denominations claim to have replaced position of Jew. No wonder Christian and Jew relationship is strained. As one Jewish scholar summed it up:

> *Thereupon they [the Christians] proclaimed themselves and the members of their churches to be the true "heirs of the promise,' applying every favorable reference and blessing to themselves and every rebuke and curse to the Jews...only the philosopher was aware of the unity of the Judeo-Christian tradition that underlies the diversity of creed and ritual.*[23]

Believers, **"...speaking the truth in love...,"** (Ephesians 4:25) can bring forth restoration in relationship with the Jew by discrediting this lie. Gentile believers have been grafted into the covenant of promise alongside Israel. The church is to, **"...share in the nourishing sap...,"** (Romans 11:17) and not become its own separate entity. Jewish objections are often based on what

[23] Jacob Bernard Agus, The Evolution of Jewish Thought (London, Abelard-Schuman, 1959), p.144

they believe a Christian believes, whether true or not. The church is not awake to the deception she is under. Many Christians, like Judas, are leading Jews against Jesus instead of to Him. He is being betrayed by his own followers like He was betrayed by Judas. Judas Iscariot led the crowd that would usher Jesus to His death. He would betray his master by a kiss. Psalm 2:12 says, **"Kiss the Son, lest he be angry and you be destroyed in your way."** A kiss is a sign of affection, but Judas, whose name means "praise" used his affection for his own interests. As noted by Alfred Edersheim, Judas not only kissed Him, but covered Him with kisses, kissed Him repeatedly, loudly, effusively.[24] Outwardly Judas showed Jesus adoration but inwardly he despised Him. Until the church forsakes the outward adoration that lacks a sincere heart, the church will only lead more Jews against Jesus. The church has not been able to catch the stumbling Jew because she herself has fallen. True holiness and sincere worship of the Messiah will make the church a powerful testimony to the unbelieving Jew.

A GREEK PHILOSOPHICAL BACKGROUND REPLACED THE JEWISH UNDERSTANDING OF THE EARLY CHURCH.

[24] Alfred Edersheim, The Life and Times of Jesus the Messiah (New York, Longmans, Green, and Co., 1906), p.543

Chapter Sixty-Eight

STUMBLING STONE

From the very beginning, Jesus was, **"a stone that causes men to stumble and a rock that makes them fall"** (2 Peter 2:8). The challenge of the early church leaders was to spread the gospel, **"...in Jerusalem, and in all Judea (Jewish evangelism) and Samaria (Samaritan evangelism) and to the ends of the earth (Gentile evangelism)"** (Acts 1:9). Each area had to have a different method
of evangelism.

After the day of Pentecost, witnessing to the Jews began, initially through Peter and this continued in Acts 1-7. Then followed Philip, who spread the gospel to the Samaritans in Acts 8-9. The continuing in Acts 10-28, evangelism to the Gentile population, beginning with Peter but mostly through Paul. Note the stages of evangelism that Jesus commanded his disciples in Acts 1:9. These stages must be seen to be an effective witness.

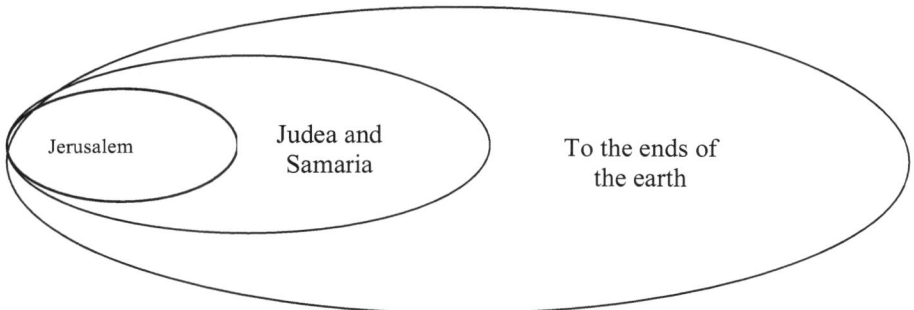

Jerusalem

Judea and Samaria

To the ends of the earth

Outreach to the traditional Jew can offer a different challenge to the believer. We must be faithful to discern the method with which to reach the Jew and not fall back upon traditional evangelistic methods. We have been promised that **"...you will receive power when the Holy Spirit comes on you; and you will be my witnesses."** Wisdom plus the power of the Holy spirit will allow effective witnessing to occur. But how has the church has failed to be the witness to the nation of Israel?

THROUGHOUT HISTORY, THE JEW WAS OFTEN GIVEN ONLY ONE OPTION; REMAIN A JEW OR BECOME A CHRISTIAN. MOST JEWISH PEOPLE COULD NOT IMAGINE REJECTING THEIR OWN IDENTITY. THE CHRISTIAN ESTABLISHMENT SHOULD NEVER HAVE SUGGESTED THAT BY BECOMING A FOLLOWER OF JESUS, A JEW WOULD DISQUALIFY HIMSELF FROM BEING A JEW. JESUS HIMSELF WAS JEWISH!

Chapter Sixty-Nine

INTOLERANCE

When the disciples of Jesus saw Judas betray their master and the crowd coming to take the Lord away, they asked, **"Lord, should we strike with our swords?"** Before allowing Jesus to respond, **"...one of them struck the servant of the high priest..."** (Luke 22:49, 50). Unfortunately, this same scenario has happened again and again throughout history whenever the Jews have rejected their Messiah. Before seeking God about how to react to the rejection of the gospel, believers have often taken up the swords against any form of resistance to Jesus's message.

Christianity began rooted in Judaism, but later became the state religion of the Roman Empire. Non-Jewish church leaders began systematically severing many of its ties with anything Jewish and sometimes even replaced it with more familiar paganistic practices. The new status that the church attained resulted in an intolerant spirit toward Judaism that Max I. Dimont speaks of in his book, Jews, God, and History:

The monopolistic character of the early Church was set. Whereas in the past the Christians had settled their sectarian differences by conciliation, they now restored to the sword to enforce religious conformity.

This intolerant spirit was not only arrogant but also ignorant of the truth concerning the Jew. Because of Christian insecurity of their position in the Messiah, the Jew and traditional Judaism became a threat. The reaction of Jesus to the raising of the word against those who rejected him was, **"No more of this!"** (Luke 22:51) But our response to His cry is too late because we the church have already swung the sword. For restored relationship, the church needs to repent of her many offenses against the Jew. If the church fails to do so, the wound will only become more infected and painful. Addressing theological barriers will help us better understand the reasons behind Jews resisting conversion and belief that Jesus is the Messiah and the other power in heaven. Speaking of the Jewish rejection of the Messiah, Paul proclaims:

But if their transgression means riches for the world, and their loss means riches for the Gentiles, how much greater riches will their fullness bring! (Romans 11:12 NIV)

Jewish conversion will bring riches to the Gentiles. Many barriers exist that hinder their salvation from coming to pass. What if the church focused mainly on converting the Jews to Jesus? Would world-wide revival then occur?

WE MUST SEEK TO REMOVE ALL BARRIERS THAT HAVE HINDERED THE JEWS FROM RECEIVING JESUS AS THE MESSIAH. JESUS HAS TO BE THE JEWISH MESSIAH, OR HE CANNOT BE ANYONE'S MESSIAH.

Chapter Seventy

ONE NEW MAN

Our God ordained one new man to come into existence after the death of Jesus. This one new man was to be made up of Jewish and Gentile believers (Ephesians 2:15). Paul's letter to the Romans in chapters 9 through 11, specifically calls out to the believers to hold on to their Jewish roots. I believe these chapters hold the answer to much of the confusion the church has with the nation of Israel. Paul seeks to correct the Roman believers in their early stages of deception. Yet deception was not only with the Gentile believers but also with the Jewish believers.

Neither the Jewish community nor the Jewish Christian community shared Paul's conception of a single community of Jews and Gentiles. The book of Acts was written primarily to deal with Jew and Gentile relationship in the Messiah, but this message fell on deaf ears. By the second century C. E., the church was composed almost entirely of Gentiles. The path of least resistance was for the Gentiles to remain a separate community from their Jewish brothers. This separation from Jewish customs and laws soon evolved into a hatred and disgust for the Jewish faith by many Christians.

Due to this separatist mentality, Jews desiring to become true followers of Jesus were expected to enter into the Gentile community and to reject everything that was Jewish. Many Jews entered into the Gentile community to become a Christian, but many others did not because of the God given call to remain Jewish. This antisemitic spirit hindered Jewish conversion in the same way Gentile conversion was hindered by the certain Jews who required them to be circumcised. Paul even confronted Peter in Galatians 2:14, **"How is it, then, that you force Gentiles to follow Jewish customs?"**

This controversy brought together the leaders of the church in the book of Acts.

Then some of the believers who belonged to the party of the Pharisees stood up and said, "The Gentiles must be circumcised and required to obey the law of Moses."
(Acts 15:5 NIV)

The Apostle Paul was instrumental at this meeting to help solve the question of incorporating both Jews and Gentiles into the faith. One writer remarked, *"Paul tried to accomplish the impossible, namely, to establish a new Israel on a foundation that could include both Jews and Gentiles"* [25]

At the end of the discourse, James, the half-brother of Jesus said:

It is my judgment, therefore, that we should not make it difficult for the Gentiles who are turning to God. Instead, we should write to them, telling them to abstain from food polluted by idols, from sexual immorality, from the meat of strangled animals and from blood. (Acts 15:19-21 NIV)

---

[25] Helmut Koester

James was proposing limited requirements for Gentiles that would allow Jew and Gentile to fellowship together as one body. Many scholars believe this is in reference to the Noahic covenant as found in Genesis 9:4-6.

Judaizers were those who thought it would be right to force circumcision on Gentiles and believed it was necessary for salvation. To Paul, it was the cross plus nothing that brought salvation. Read Galatians 2 to hear Paul's frustration with the Judaizers and Peter. Parts of the Law became optional to Gentiles but not forced. Paul writes in his letters to the churches often on his view of certain Old Testament assumptions on lifestyle. Paul is never suggesting that the moral law is invalidated– only the ceremonial law. When Paul is negative about the law, it is about anyone relying on the law for salvation. Below are listed some of the main issues in dealing with how a Jewish Christian ought to live and how a Gentile Christian may live.

1. Circumcision

Yet not even Titus, who was with me, was compelled to be circumcised, even though he was a Greek. (Galatians 2:3 NIV)

2. Observance of Sabbaths and Holidays

Therefore do not let anyone judge you by what you eat or drink, or with regard to a religious festival, a New Moon celebration, or a Sabbath day. (Colossians 2:16 NIV)

3. Dietary Laws

The man who eats everything must not look down on

193

him who does not, and the man who does not eat everything must not condemn the man who does, for God has accepted him. (Romans 14:3 NIV)

Notice that Titus, who was not considered Jewish was not circumcised though Jewish Timothy was circumcised after his conversion (Acts 16:1-3).These were some of the lifestyle issues that Paul addressed but later many theological issues became more predominant.

OUR DOCTRINE FORMS A FOUNDATION AND SYSTEM OF BELIEFS FROM WHICH WE LIVE. THOUGH I VALUE PRAXEOLOGY (WHAT WE PRACTICE) , OVER THEOLOGY (DOCTRINES WE ADHERE TO) , I SEE THAT BOTH ARE TIED TOGETHER. TEACHING SOUND DOCTRINE WILL CONTRIBUTE TO GOOD PRACTICES. CLARITY IN WHAT WE TEACH WILL CAUSE US TO VALUE THAT WHICH GOD VALUES MOST. MY PARADIGM TELLS ME THAT GOD VALUES RELATIONSHIP OVER ' RIGHTNESS ' AND PEOPLE OVER RULES. FROM THIS PERSPECTIVE WE CAN REACH THE WORLD IN WHICH WE LIVE WITH THE LOVE OF THE FATHER AND GIVE OUR LIVES FOR THE GOSPEL OF JESUS CHRIST. THE WORLD NEEDS TO KNOW JESUS BECAUSE HE IS THE WAY BACK TO THE FATHER.

Chapter Seventy-One

ANTI-SEMITISM

The purpose of the church as is related to Israel has been severely distorted throughout history. The following is a part of a tract written by the founder of the Protestant movement, Martin Luther, in A. D. 1543:

When then shall we Christians do with this damned, rejected race of the Jews?... Let me give you my honest advice: First, to set fire to their synagogues or schools and bury and cover with dirt whatever will not burn. This is to be done in honor of our Lord and of Christendom. Second, I advise that their houses also be razed and destroyed...Third I advise that all their prayer books and Talmudic writings, in which is idolatry, lies, cursing, and blasphemy are taught, be taken from them.[26]

Luther is an example of a man who, although a brilliant scholar and great reformer, was blinded by an anti-Semitic spirit. He was probably influenced by the sins of his forefathers, who similarly persecuted the Jews in the name of Christianity. The German born monk planted seeds of hate which were later used by Hitler himself in justifying his murderous crimes against the Jewish people.

Victor Buksbazen in his book, <u>The Feasts of Israel</u>, makes

---

[26] Hal Lindsey, <u>The Road to Holocaust</u> (New York: Bantam Books, 1989), p.23

this statement concerning the blinding obsession of anti-Semitism over their accusers:

The Jew in their imagination is behind everything. All their own personal problems and frustrations, all international complexities, and human woes, all that ever went wrong, is due to the Jew- the serpent in the fool's paradise.[27]

But is this persecution from our God as judgment on the Jewish people for rejecting the Messiah? Was it not the Jewish people who said, **"Let his blood be on us and on our children?"** (Matthew 27:25). It could be said that Jewish-hatred is supernatural– but it is not from heaven. The source of this hatred is found in the pits of hell.

The devil himself is the power behind anti-Semitism. This hatred serves two purposes. First, to keep a curse upon the Gentiles, for the Lord said, **"...whoever curses you, I will curse"** (Genesis 12:3). Secondly, and more importantly, it drives a wedge between the Jews and their Messiah. Paul magnified his ministry to the Gentiles in hope to, **"...arouse my own people to envy and save some of them"** (Romans 11:14 NIV).

As the Jews have failed the plan of our God to accept the Messiah, so the Gentiles have failed the plan of our God to reflect the Messiah. Satan's plan is to hinder God's purpose for the Jew and Gentile as described in Ephesians 2:16, **"His purpose was to create in himself one new man out of the two, thus making**

---

[27] Victor Bukshazen, The Feasts of Israel (Fort Washington, PA: Christian Literature Crusade, Inc., 1954), p.75

peace." This can only happen through Christ:

For he himself is our peace, who has made the two one (Jew and Gentile) and has destroyed the barrier, the dividing wall of hostility (Ephesians 2:14 NIV)

Yet this wall of hostility has remained because of the Church's persecution upon the Jewish people.

In the view of the history of Jewish persecution by Christians, what should the Gentile response be? Let the wall of hostility be brought down and pursue the mystery of the Gentile and Jew in one body. Both arrogance and willful ignorance are sins to be reckoned with and be repented of so as to obtain the full measure of grace we need at this hour.

Our culture has little to no understanding of the "One New Man" concept. Jews and Christians are seen as opposing forces in the mindset of most believers, yet this was not so in the early church. You could not be a Christian unless you were Jewish! It was not until about ten years after the death and resurrection of Christ that anyone even thought otherwise. After Peter's vision of unclean animals and his divine appointment with Cornelius, he said in astonishment: **"I now realize how true it is that our God does not show favoritism"** (Acts 10:34 TNT). This was revelation to Peter! What began with Jews doubting Gentiles would be able to receive Christ "as Gentiles," transformed into Gentiles doubting that Jews would be able to receive Christ "as Jews." First there was Jews persecuting Christians then Christians persecuting Jews.

Satan has purposed to keep "the wall of hostility" high

and unscalable. We must do our best to do the opposite. In the next chapter, the doctrine of dispensationalism will be described as well as its anti-Semitic nature.

JESUS CAME TO THE JEWISH PEOPLE BEING BORN A JEW. INITIALLY, HE MOSTLY REJECTED MINISTERING TO GENTILES SAYING, "I WAS SENT ONLY TO THE LOST SHEEP OF ISRAEL." (MATTHEW 15:24) REMEMBER THAT ALL OF JESUS' FOLLOWERS WERE JEWISH AND THE ENTIRE NEW TESTAMENT WAS WRITTEN BY JEWS, EXCEPT FOR LUKE, ACTS AND POSSIBLY THE BOOK OF HEBREWS. JESUS REVEALED HIMSELF TO THE JEWS AND EXPECTED THEM TO TAKE THE GOSPEL, FROM THEIR PERSPECTIVE, TO THE WORLD. IN THEIR CULTURE, THE JEWS HAVE AN INGRAINED UNDERSTANDING OF THE FATHER'S BLESSING. THEY HAVE A GIFT AND REVELATION OF THE POWER OF 'BLESSING' THAT GOES FROM GENERATION TO GENERATION. IF WE SAY 'YES' TO JESUS, BUT 'NO' TO OUR JEWISH ROOTS, WE LOSE PART OF OUR SPIRITUAL INHERITANCE. WE KNOW THAT JEWS AS A PEOPLE GROUP, HAVE REJECTED JESUS AS THE MESSIAH. IN TURN, THIS HAS CAUSED MUCH OF OUR OWN CHRISTIAN THEOLOGY TO BE LACKING.

Chapter Seventy-Two

DISPENSATIONALISM

A doctrine that is prevalent in the church today is called "dispensationalism". At the heart of this doctrine is the dividing of all time into distinguishable economics (or dispensations) which are seen in God's progressive revelation.[28] C.I. Scofield (1834-1921 AD), author of the highly influential Scofield Reference Bible(1909 AD) described a dispensation as a period of time during which man is tested in respect of obedience to some specific revelation of the will of God.[29] John Nelson Darby (1800-1882 AD) was the first to create an elaborate interpretation of these dispensations.

In Darby's interpretation, he sees two distinct plans of our God: one concerning Israel and one concerning the church. Because Israel rejected the Messiah, our God turned away from Israel and made for Himself a new people out of the Gentiles. According to the postponement theory, our God will not resume his dealings with Israel until He finishes building the church and raptures it up to heaven.[30]

From Darby's dispensationalism comes the doctrine of the pre-tribulation rapture. Far from having its roots in the early

---

[28] Dictionary of Christianity in America (Madison, WI: InterVarsity Press, 1990), p.358
[29] Ibid, p.358
[30] Ibid, 358

199

church, the pretribulation rapture and an any-moment Rapture can trace its origin back to John Darby and the Plymouth Brethren in the year 1830.[31] This view claims that the church will be raptured before the tribulation period and the poor Jew will be left behind.

There is a divisive effect that these doctrines have upon the relationship between the Jew and Gentile. What Jesus did to **"...destroy the barrier, the dividing wall of hostility..."**, dispensationalism had erected another in its place. It is not the will of God for Jews and Gentiles to be divided. Our God desires them to unite together for His divine purpose.

If God has rejected the Jew for this dispensation than the Jew is purposeless until the next age. As Hal Lindsay writes in his book, The Road to Holocaust, when the church began to see itself as God's true Israel, the inheritor of the covenant promises made to Israel, then in the eyes of the church, the Israelites ceased to have any legitimate purpose or right to exist as a people.[32] Dispensationalism, in the wrong hands will become a doctrine of anti-Semitism. Many strong leaders have blindly embraced this view without realizing the seeds of anti-Semitism being sown. The nation of Israel must be understood in light of this because if she is not in her rightful position all nations will be at stake.

---

[31] Rosenthal/Howard, Examining the Pre-Wrath Rapture of the Church (Nashville: Thomas Nelson Publishers, 1994), p.119
[32] Lindsey, p.9

Chapter Seventy-Three

PROPHET LIKE MOSES

There is a warning in Deuteronomy 13 against false prophets that has in the past been applied to Jesus. The warning states:

If a prophet, or one who foretells by dreams, appears among you, and announces to you a miraculous sign or wonder, and if the sign or wonder of which he has spoken takes place, and he says, "Let us follow other gods" (gods you have not known) "and let us worship them," you must not listen to the words of that prophet or dreamer. (Deuteronomy 13:1-3 NIV) The Gospels are full of accounts of Jesus performing miraculous signs and wonders that have come to pass. It is scriptural not to follow Him or anyone for that reason alone. Where Jesus proves not to be the false prophet that He does not encourage people to follow other gods. Jesus said, **"Do not think that I have come to abolish the Law or the Prophets: I have not come to abolish them but to fulfill them."** (Matthew 5:17 NIV)

Unfortunately, the church has failed to set this same example. For a Jew to walk into a cathedral and see statues of Mary and other figures, this is idolatry. Deuteronomy 5:8 says, **"You shall not make for yourself an idol in the form of anything in heaven above or on the earth beneath or in the waters below."** Followers of Jesus have not been spared from the same error that Aaron made when he formed the golden

201

calves.

Jesus is not a false prophet because he has led millions of people thought the world to worship the God of Israel. He has not brought them to "other gods".

In Deuteronomy 18, the LORD spoke to Moses concerning the Prophet. The Prophet and the Messiah were not necessarily considered one in the same, but clearly Jesus fulfilled the following scripture in which the LORD is speaking to Moses:

I will raise up for them a prophet like you from among their brothers; I will put my words in his mouth, and he will tell them everything I command him. If anyone does not listen to my words that the prophet speaks in my name, I myself will call him to account. (Deuteronomy 18:18-19 NIV)

The key to defining who the Prophet will be is that He will be like Moses. Throughout the passage, the singular use of the word prophet is used. No other prophet from among the Israelites has risen to compare with Jesus.

Moses worked great miracles which had national impact. Though Elijah and Elisha were also miracle workers, they did not leave a legacy of bringing their nation into legal covenant like Moses. To be a prophet like Moses, Jesus alone can compare. After the feeding of the five thousand, the people said of Jesus, **"Surely this is the Prophet who is to come into the world."** (John 6:14 NIV)

Moses was a lawgiver, covenant maker and teacher. His teachings carried great authority over the people unlike no other Old Testament prophet. As Moses brought a people into covenant with God, so Jesus brought a people into covenant with God through His own blood (Luke 22:20 NIV). No other teacher has such profound influence upon Jewish thought since the time of Moses. Moses was a deliverer and mediator. What other prophet delivered masses of people from bondage (Exodus 13) and stood between God and the people as a mediator, fasting forty days and forty nights? (Deuteronomy 9:18) What other Jewish figure ever offered up his life, as in Deuteronomy 32:32, **"But now, please forgive their sin– but if not, then blot me out of the book you have written."** May all of Israel say, like the Jews who heard Jesus at the feast of Tabernacles: **"Surely this man is the Prophet"** (John 7:40 NIV). Jesus said, **"For if you believed Moses, you would believe me; for he wrote of me"** (John 5:46 ESV)

HISTORICALLY, THE CHURCH HAS PROVOKED ISRAEL, BUT NOT TO JEALOUSY. SAINT AUGUSTINE, WHO WAS ONE OF THE MOST INFLUENTIAL THEOLOGIANS IN OUR CHRISTIAN HERITAGE, SAID OF THE JEWS IN HIS DAY, "LET THEM LIVE AMONG US, BUT LET THEM SUFFER AND BE CONTINUALLY HUMILIATED."[33] AUGUSTINE PLANTED A SEED OF ANTI-SEMITISM THAT WOULD LATER PRODUCE A HARVEST OF BLOODSHED OF JEWS.

[33] "The Guilt of Christianity Towards the Jewish People - Anti-Semitism and Holocaust." *Christian Action for Israel*. Web. 18 Dec. 2010.

Chapter Seventy-Four

BOOK OF ENOCH

The Bible is the most quoted book in history. But did you know that the Bible quotes other writings? The Book of Enoch is quoted in the book of Jude 14-15 which is found in the New Testament. Here is a portion of the Book of Enoch 48:2-3 where the Son of Man is mentioned, as described in Daniel chapter 2.

And in that hour that Son of Man was named in the presence of the Lord of Spirits, and his name, before the Head of Days. Even before the sun and the constellations were created, before the stars of heaven were made, his name was named before the Lord of Spirits.

The Son of Man is manifested in the person of Jesus. This figure in the book of Enoch allowed the Jewish people to understand who Jesus was and how they ought to respond to Him.

And he will be the light of the nations, and he will be a hope for those who grieve in their hearts. All who dwell on the earth will fall down and worship before him, and they will glorify and bless and sing hymns to the name of the Lord of Spirits... for in his name they are saved, and he is the vindicator of their lives.(Enoch 48:4-7)

This Son of Man will be worshipped on earth and in His name, those on earth will be saved and vindicated.

And they had great joy, and they blessed and glorified and exalted, because the name of that son of man had been revealed to them. And he sat on the throne of glory and the whole judgment was given to the

Son of Man, and he will make sinners vanish and perish from the face of the earth. (Enoch 69:26-27)

And in Enoch 69:29, he will return to earth to judge the world.

And he has sat down on the throne of his glory, and all evil will vanish from his presence. And the word of the Son of Man will go forth and will prevail in the presence of the Lord of Spirits.

The Son of Man is seated at the right hand of the Ancient of Days. The conclusion must be that the Son of Man is in fact a second person. And all of the functions assigned to the divine figure called "one like a son of man" in Daniel 7 are given to this Son of Man, who is also called, as we have seen, the Christ.

The 3rd century church father Tertullian compares the Old Testament references to the "Son of Man" with the New Testament "Son of Man' sayings of Jesus to show that the Old Testament did, indeed, foretell the coming of Christ.[34] Unfortunately, many Jews did not perceive the other power in heaven was the Son of Man in the book of Daniel. Jesus used this title in hopes that deaf ears would hear.

The church needs to fully understand the role of Jesus as found in the Old Testament. His appearances bring a strong case

---

[34] "..because He wanted, by help of the very designation "Son of Man" from the book of Daniel, so to induce them to reflect as to show them that He who remitted sins was... indeed, in the prophecy of Daniel, who had obtained the power of judging, and thereby, of course, of forgiving sins likewise (for He who judges also absolves); so that, when once that objection of theirs [3804] was shattered to pieces by their recollection of Scripture, they might the more easily acknowledge Him to be the Son of man Himself by His own actual forgiveness of sins. Tertullian. The Complete Works of Tertullian (33 Books With Active Table of Contents) . Kindle Edition.

of His role as the Messiah. Peter yielded the sword, but the church must yield to the Spirit.

When Peter cut off the ear of the servant who rejected his Messiah, he prophetically announced what was to occur in the future of the church. Peter's reaction resulted in a wounded man in pain and a bloody ear on the ground. This is a picture of where the church and the Jew stand today. The striking of the sword cut off the hearing capacity of the one who needs to hear. It is time we step back and allow Jesus to heal the wounded ear of our Jewish brother. His normal pattern of healing required faith on the part of the one who needed healing, but this is not the case. May Jesus again pick up the wounded ear and restore it to the ones in need of healing. **"And He touched the man's ear and healed him."** (Luke 22:51 NIV)

JESUS IS THE ROCK THAT WILL MAKE MAN STUMBLE. BUT WHEN A JEW STUMBLES, THEY MAY LACK THE FULL UNDERSTANDING OF THE MESSAGE. AS CHRISTIANS, WE HAVE A RESPONSIBILITY TO EXPLAIN WHAT WE BELIEVE IN ORDER TO BRING UNDERSTANDING. LISTEN TO THE PARABLE OF THE SOWER: "WHEN ANYONE HEARS THE MESSAGE ABOUT THE KINGDOM AND DOES NOT UNDERSTAND IT, THE EVIL ONE COMES AND SNATCHES AWAY WHAT WAS SOWN IN HIS HEART" (MATTHEW 13:19)

Chapter Seventy-Five

INDESTRUCTIBLE JEW

History is full of great civilizations. Only one has survived to the extent of the Jews. Without land for two thousand years, with only the traditions of their forefathers, they have not only remained a people but have flourished into a nation. Throughout the diaspora and through numerous persecutions, the Jew has continued to impact on history. This influence can only be the hand of our God. But why? God's hand has been upon the Jew throughout His-story and what His purpose is by preserving the Jewish people. A wake-up call is needed for the church to honor her roots so that it may go well with her, and she may enjoy a long life.

Dead bodies that are preserved are called mummies. This process was done because the people of ancient Egypt believed that the deceased would come to life again.[35] Our God has also preserved a people that will come to life again. Our God values what He preserves, and He preserves for a purpose. History proves this fact.

Most great nations of history, which appeared at the same time the Jews did, have disappeared.[36] The Chinese, Hindus, and

---

[35] The World Book Encyclopedia (Chicago: Field Enterprises Educational Corporation, 1959), p.5331

[36] Max I. Dimont, Jews, God and History (New York: The New American Library, Inc., 1962), p. 15

Egyptian peoples are the only ones living today who are as old as the Jewish people.[37] But unlike the Jews, these civilizations were never driven from their land and oppressed in foreign territories. Hence, the basis for their survival could be traced to the security of their land. Never were these peoples thrown amid countercultures, which tested the very foundations of their faith. The Jews not only survived in these cultures but significantly impacted the civilizations that sought to destroy them.

Jewish ideas now govern two-thirds of the civilized world.[38] Yet Jewish people make up less than .003% of the world's population![39] Amazingly, 12% of all the Nobel prizes in physics, chemistry, and medicine have been awarded to those of Jewish descent.[40] Influential thinkers like Albert Einstein, Sigmund Freud, and Karl Marx have had phenomenal sway over how modern man think– and yes, they are all Jewish! Has God put something in their very being that they influence those around them by nature? It can hardly be contested.

Paul says of Israel, **"for God's gifts are irrevocable"** (Romans 11:29). The Greek word for irrevocable is a negative form of the world *metamellomai*. This word means to care afterwards.[41] The negative of this would be not care after the gift

---

[37] Ibid, p.15
[38] Ibid, p.421
[39] Michael Brown, Our Hands Are Stained With Blood (Shippensburg, PA: Destiny Image Publishers, 1992), p.84
[40] Dimont, p.14
[41] James Strong, Strong's Exhaustive Concordance of the Bible (Abingdon: World Bible Publishers, 1980), p.63

is given. This Scripture means God gifts the Jews to be an influence throughout the earth, even if their impact goes against their Maker.

Their gifting to be a powerful influence upon the Gentiles has never left the Jewish people. In Isaiah 49:6, we read, **"I will make you a light for the Gentiles...".** They have been a light to the Gentiles worldwide since their conception, but their purpose has been misunderstood. The advancement of technology, the arts, and sciences are not their true calling but instead, "...that you may bring my salvation to the ends of the earth." To see their purpose, we must first see their beginnings.

AT THE TIME JESUS CAME TO EARTH, THE JEWS WERE DEVOUT IN FOLLOWING THE LAW OF MOSES. BUT INSTEAD OF DRAWING THEM CLOSER TO YAHWEH, IT BECAME A SYSTEM OF 'DOING,' WITHOUT ANY REAL NEED FOR RELATIONSHIP. I CALL IT "DO-IT-YOURSELF" SALVATION. PERFORMANCE-BASED ACCEPTANCE EMPHASIZES RULES OVER RELATIONSHIP. PERFORMANCE DRIVEN PEOPLE CONTINUALLY TRY TO FOLLOW THE RULES SO THAT THEY CAN EXPERIENCE THE ACCEPTANCE OF THEIR HEAVENLY FATHER, INSTEAD OF RESTING IN THE ACCEPTANCE THAT IS FOUND IN JESUS' BLOOD SACRIFICE.

Chapter Seventy-Six

FATHER ABRAHAM

About the year 2000 B.C.E., our God spoke to a man by the name of Abram, who was later called Abraham. These are the words our God spoke:

Leave your country, your people, and your father's household and go to the land I will show you. I will make your name great, and you will be a blessing, I will bless those who bless you, and whoever curses you, I will curse; and all people on earth will be blessed through you. (Genesis 12:1-3 NIV)

Note that seven promises God gave to Abram:

(1) "I will make you into a great nation,"

(2) "I will bless you,"

(3) "I will make your name great,"

(4) "You will be a blessing,"

(5) "I will bless those who bless you,"

(6) "whoever curses you, I will curse,"

(7) "all people on earth will be blessed by you."

This covenant was the first of many our God made with man. Yet this covenant holds significance because it was Yahweh taking the next step in redeeming humankind.

In essence, Abraham became the high priest of the earth, a representative of all humanity. He was to walk out the promises God gave him in faith. Although God's covenant is unconditional, individual members must exercise their faith and obedience to reap the benefits. Our God will not break His covenant but will require faith on behalf of the covenant partner. As it is written, **"Abram believed the Lord, and he credited it to Him as righteousness."** (Genesis 15:6). Through his faith and obedience, Abraham opened the door for all the peoples of the earth to be blessed.

The covenant our God made with Abraham was truly dependent upon His grace. What one-hundred-year-old man could cause his ninety-year-old wife to have a child? Divine empowerment or grace is the basis of all the covenants our God makes with man. Grace in the western mindset means unmerited favor with the stress placed on our un-deservingness and not His favor. But the true meaning of grace is the empowerment given to us to fulfill His covenant as promised.

In John 8:31-41, we can see it was common for Jews to say of themselves, **"We are Abraham's descendants..."** (John 8:33). Their attachment to Abraham is based on the promises made to him concerning his descendants. These covenants were the foundations that gave rise to a will to survive as Jews, which has been the driving force in Judaism. Even Ezra commanded the Jewish men guilty of intermarriage, **"...to send away all these women and their children..."** breaking up families to preserve their race. But the resistance to assimilating into other cultures should be seen in light of the covenants made with Abraham.

211

Chapter Seventy-Seven

PROMISE TO NATIONS

In due time, the chain of promises which began with Abraham in Ur of Chaldees will find its wonderful culmination in the coming again of Messiah Jesus. The Jewish people were the soil where the Messiah would sprout, and Abraham was the first of the Hebrews. His lineage connects him with the Messiah in a privileged way, as is evident in the account of Abraham sacrificing Isaac. Genesis 22 foreshadows the very act in which salvation would come to all the peoples of the earth. A Father and Son work together to establish salvation for the entire world.

Many parallels can be made between Isaac and the Lord Jesus. Isaac patiently bore the wood for his own sacrifice, and he submitted to his sacrifice without resistance. This moment was undoubtedly Abraham's most difficult trial, as the Cross would be for Yahweh generations later. When our God tested Abraham by having him offer Isaac as a sacrifice, Abraham gave up the natural means by which the covenant promise would be established. But he acted in faith and **"...reasoned that God could raise the dead."** (Hebrews 11:19). But as he reached out his hand to slay his son, he was stopped by the Angel of the Lord. Abraham was promised numerous descendants, who were given possession of enemy lands, and that **"...through your offspring, all nations on earth would be blessed, because**

you have obeyed me" (Genesis 22:18 NIV). This act of obedience was not just playing out of the Messiah's sacrifice, but it was an act that prophetically summoned our Heavenly Father to send His Only Son. Understand the profound effect of one man's obedience upon all humanity– a turning point in mankind's relationship with God.

Isaac was later to father two children, Jacob and Esau. Our God loved Jacob but hated Esau. Through Jacob came twelve sons, and through these twelve sons came twelve tribes. But during a time of famine, Jacob and his sons were forced into the land of Egypt. For four hundred years, they lived there, mistreated, and enslaved by the Egyptians. But our God promised Abraham, **"I will punish the nation they serve as slaves, and afterwards, they will come out with great possessions"** (Genesis 15:14). Out of Egypt would come a nation of enslaved people, which would become the nation of Israel.

It is interesting to note that the Lord said Israel was chosen, **"....not because of your righteousness or your integrity..."** (Deuteronomy 9:5). This clan of enslaved people was not becoming holier and holier throughout those four hundred years of slavery in Egypt, as our God waited for them to attain some form of righteousness. Instead, he said to Abraham, **"in the fourth generation, your descendants will come back here (Canaan), for the sin of the Amorites has not yet reached its full measure"** (Genesis 5:6). He was not waiting for the Jews to become holier but instead for the Amorites' sin to reach full measure so he could expel them.

Chapter Seventy-Eight

MOSAIC COVENANT

At the appointed time, Moses was raised up and delivered the people from the hand of Pharaoh. Through Moses, another covenant was made called the Mosaic covenant. This covenant was a temporary administration of God's grace until the New Covenant could be established.

The Purpose of the Mosaic Covenant

1. First, it was to set standards of conduct and morality for the Jews. Law and order were necessary to protect the Israelites from being defiled by other influences. This covenant included many safety and sanitation procedures and spiritual matters because our God wanted these people to remain healthy and holy. Their preservation as a people was necessary, and the lack of law and order would endanger their very existence.

2. Secondly, it was to set them apart from other nations. In Deuteronomy 4:6, the Lord tells the Jews concerning the Mosaic laws: **"Observe them carefully, for this will show your wisdom and understanding to the nations, who will hear about these decrees and say, 'Surely this great nation is a wise and understanding people.'"** The Jews were to be recognized as different. Their differences were to bring the interests of other nations to them in the hope that they would also come to salvation through the Messiah.

214

3. Thirdly, this covenant put into effect a sacrificial system that places Israel in the role of an intercessor for all nations. The blood that was poured out of the bulls and goats cried out to God to withhold judgment from the nations of the earth and Israel itself until the Messiah would come to redeem them. Israel's purpose as a mediator between our God and all nations still exists today. Our God has never given up on His purpose of preserving a nation among the nations to demonstrate His lordship.

Many believe that the church is now the spiritual Israel. Yet our God will not break His promises to Israel to avoid offending the church. Israel is the nation to represent all nations before our God– a role that the church cannot fulfill.

IN THE BOOK OF ISAIAH, HE SPEAKS OF A TIME WHEN GENTILES WILL PROCLAIM A RESTING PLACE FOR THE JEWISH PEOPLE. BUT BECAUSE THE JEW WOULD NOT LISTEN, THE WORD OF THE LORD TO THEM WOULD NOT RESULT IN FREEDOM. "WITH FOREIGN LIPS AND STRANGE TONGUES GOD WILL SPEAK TO THIS PEOPLE, TO WHOM HE SAID, 'THIS IS THE RESTING PLACE, LET THE WEARY REST,' AND, 'THIS IS THE PLACE OF REPOSE' –BUT THEY WOULD NOT LISTEN."
(ISAIAH 28:11–12 NIV)

Chapter Seventy-Nine

ISRAEL'S CALL

Our God never intended to be the God of only one nation. Not to single out Israel as the best but as a tool of redemption for all nations. The goal is this: **"All nations will come and worship before You"** (Revelation 15:4 NIV). In the soon future, redeemed Israel will say of Jesus, **"Blessed is He who comes in the name of the Lord"** (Matthew 23:39 NIV)

The purpose of Israel being formed is fourfold:
1. **To be an intercessor for the nations**
2. **To be a picture of redemption**
3. **To be an example to the other nations**
4. **To be a means of preparing the world for the Messiah.**

Have you ever wondered what would have happened if Jesus had come to Russia or Africa two thousand years ago? No one would have been waiting for Him. What other people could Jesus of come through?

The Hebrew Scriptures, prayers, sacrifices, and celebrations were, in essence, the formal invitation to the Messiah, saying, **"Come, Lord Jesus"** (Revelation 22:20). The Jews were the nation that would **"...prepare the way for the LORD; make straight in the wilderness a highway for our God"** (Isaiah 40:3 NIV).

The restoration of the nation of Israel and her conversion

directly correlates to the second coming of Christ. Jesus says of Jerusalem, **"...you will not see me again until you say, 'Blessed is he who comes in the name of the Lord"** (Matthew 23:39 NIV). Peter preaches to his fellow Jews a similar message, **"Repent, then, and turn to God... that he may send the Christ"** (Acts 3:19,20 NIV). Satan knows that their repentance will bring forth Christ and also his judgment. With this in mind, we can better understand why the enemy has sought to keep Jews out of Israel and keep them bitter against Christianity.

THE WORD REPENT IS THE GREEK WORD METANOE, WHICH MEANS TO CHANGE YOUR PARADIGM. META MEANS 'CHANGE' AND NOE MEANS 'MIND' OR 'WAY OF THINKING.' YET MOST PEOPLE THINK OF REPENTANCE, IN THE CONTEXT OF, FIRST, HAVING AN EMOTIONAL RESPONSE TO THEIR SIN, AND SECONDLY, TURNING AWAY FROM THEIR UNGODLY LIFESTYLE. TRUE REPENTANCE CAUSES US TO GO TO A HIGHER PLACE, VIEWING LIFE FROM GOD'S PERSPECTIVE INSTEAD OF OUR OWN. REMEMBER THAT JESUS SAID THAT REPENTANCE, OR A PARADIGM SHIFT IS REQUIRED BEFORE YOU CAN BELIEVE. "THE TIME HAS COME," HE SAID. "THE KINGDOM OF GOD IS NEAR. REPENT AND BELIEVE THE GOOD NEWS!" (MARK 1:15)

Chapter Eighty

JOSEPH'S ASCENSION

There is a striking parallel between Joseph's life and the Messiah's return to Israel. Joseph is a type of Christ, and his brothers are a picture of the nation of Israel. Joseph's father loved him more than any of his other brothers. His father's special love for him and the dream Joseph had about all his family bowing down and worshipping him stirred jealousy amongst his brothers. This jealousy and hatred toward Joseph eventually led him to be sold by his brothers as a slave. Then he was brought into Egypt.

Jesus was also highly beloved by His Father. The thought of Jesus calling God "Father" stirred jealousy and anger amongst the Jews. When the crowds began to worship him when he entered Jerusalem during the passion week, this infuriated the religious Jews, making them even more determined to kill him. By the end of that week, Jesus' Jewish brothers handed him over to Roman authority to be crucified. Just like Jesus resurrected spiritually, Joseph resurrected socially and politically. By interpreting a dream of Pharaoh, he received the highest position in Egypt next only to Pharaoh himself. Pharaoh told him:

You shall be in charge of my palace, and all my people are to submit to you. Only with respect to the throne will I be

218

greater than you. (Genesis 41:40 NIV).

Joseph entered Egypt as a slave but, within a few years, achieved the highest position of power in the world. A famine spread over the whole country, and Joseph's brothers, living in Canaan, were forced to come to Egypt to buy grain. When they arrived, Joseph recognized them, but they did not recognize Joseph. He spoke harshly to them, but it was in his heart to have his family restored to him. Our God brought Joseph's brothers to a place where they depended on him for mercy. There was no hope for them outside of the hand of Joseph. A similar scenario will soon happen to Israel. They will be in a desperate place as **"...all the nations of the earth are gathered against her"** (Zechariah 12:3 NIV). Yet this is what "...the leaders of Judah will say in their hearts, **'The people of Jerusalem are strong because the LORD Almighty is their God"** (Zechariah 12:5 NIV). They will acknowledge their total dependence upon the Lord in this desperate situation.

JOSEPH TRUSTED OUR GOD AND STAYED FAITHFUL AND RECEIVED A GREAT REWARD. OUR GOD USED THE WICKEDNESS OF JOSEPH'S BROTHERS TO BRING HIM INTO A POSITION TO RULE A NATION. JOSEPH NEVER BECAME A VICTIM OF HIS CIRCUMSTANCES BUT CONTINUED TO BE FAITHFUL TO HIS GOD AND FAITHFUL TO PUT HIS BEST EFFORT FORTH IN EVERY SITUATION.

Chapter Eighty-One

JOSEPH UNVEILED

Joseph was very subtle when dealing with his brothers. He put them in a place of vulnerability to see how they would respond. These were the people who had given him up to death! At the high point in the account of his dealings with his brothers, Joseph accuses the youngest brother Benjamin of stealing a silver cup. They had vowed beforehand that whoever had the cup would be bound to Joseph forever, though the cup was placed in Benjamin's bag by Joseph's servants and was not stolen. Judah, the wicked brother who sold Joseph into slavery, stepped forward at this point. He begged Joseph to allow Benjamin to go free and to take him as his slave instead. At this point, Joseph broke down in tears and revealed himself to his brothers. He wept over them and embraced them. Oh, the surprise of his brothers! They had done such evil to Joseph, yet he forgave them. It is a beautiful account of the restoration of our God and His eternal love.

Similarly, Jesus will veil Himself to the Jews in their time of desperation to see what is in their hearts. Judah is a picture of Israel, and Benjamin is a picture of the church. Judah had once sold his younger brother out of jealousy, but the new Judah gave himself for his brother. Will the old Israel be willing to give herself over as the representative she is called to be? Will she step in as the mediator for all nations? But at the height of their desperation, Jesus will unveil Himself as their Messiah. Israel will be even more shaken than the brothers of Joseph were! And once this happens, Zechariah 12:10 will be fulfilled:

And I will pour out on the house of David and the inhabitants of Jerusalem a spirit of grace and supplication. They will look on me, the one they have pierced, and they will mourn for him as one mourns for an only child and grieve bitterly for him as one grieves for a firstborn son.

The book of Zechariah is full of the words of Angel-Yahweh– Jesus revealing Himself in the Old Testament. The other power in heaven is speaking, and we must shout his words to the Jewish people. The coming of the Messiah into Jerusalem and back to the Jews will bring fulfillment to the covenants of old– for the glory of God, who fulfills all of His promises.

MOST OF US THINK OF THE FUTURE AS AHEAD OF US. HEBRAIC THOUGHT SEES THE PAST IN FRONT OF US, AND WE ARE BACKING INTO THE FUTURE, SIMILAR TO A PERSON ROWING A ROWBOAT. WE ARE LOOKING BACK AT OUR HISTORY AS WE MOVE INTO THE UNSEEN PROMISES OF OUR FUTURE.

Chapter Eighty-Two

SELF-PERSECUTION

Understanding how the church could persecute the Jew is like comprehending a branch taking an ax, and swinging it at the roots of its very own roots! The other trees in the forest would say to the branch, "What are you doing? Don't you know that you are destroying your own being and endangering your very existence?" The branch's actions would be utterly foolish. Yet the church, like this branch, has taken this very stance toward its roots, the Jewish people.

The Apostle Paul made a parallel between the Gentile church and the branches of a tree and the Jewish people and tree roots. We can see in this parallel how the church has failed. Paul says to the Gentiles, **"You do not support the root, but the root supports you"** (Romans 11;18 NIV). In the next verse, Paul writes, **"Do not be arrogant, but be afraid"** (Romans 11:19 NIV). Seeing the church in this dependent relationship with its Jewish roots is a humbling truth.

In these verses in Romans 11, Paul seems to be dealing with anti-Semitic attitudes in the Church of Rome. Arrogance and ignorance of these truths throughout history have been shocking. The proud church refuses to submit to this relationship and has arrogantly proclaimed the judgment of God upon the Jew. Yes, some of their distress has been the direct judgment of God, but the church should be afraid when such things occur. Paul warns the Roman church: **"For if God did not spare the natural branches, he will not spare you either"** (Romans 11:21 NIV).

ISAIAH 28 ALLUDES TO THE PEOPLE OF ISRAEL "...WILL GO AND FALL BACKWARD, BE INJURED AND SNARED AND CAPTURED." A SNARE IS SOMETHING METAPHORICALLY THAT ALLURES ONE FROM HIS REAL PURPOSE AND THEN DESTROYS HIM.[42] WHEN WE THINK WE CAN ATTAIN RIGHTEOUSNESS THROUGH OUR OWN WORKS IT BECOMES A SNARE TO US! BUT JUST LIKE IT HAPPENED TO MANY JEWS IN THE TIME OF JESUS, BEWARE THAT IT DOES NOT HAPPEN TO YOU! WE MUST NOT LET THE WORD OF THE LORD BECOME "DO AND DO AND RULE ON RULE" AND REFUSE TO ENTER HIS REST. JESUS LITERALLY BECAME THE SABBATH REST FOR HIS PEOPLE AND OUR WORK IS NOT FOR SALVATION BUT FROM SALVATION. WE MUST END OUR STRIVING FOR RIGHTEOUSNESS, AND LEARN TO SIMPLY AND FULLY RECEIVE IT.

---

[42] Harris, R. Laird, Gleason L. Archer, and Bruce K. Waltke. *Theological Wordbook of the Old Testament.* Chicago: Moody, 1980. 399. Print.

Chapter Eighty-Three

GRAFTED IN

Paul said of the Gentile church, **"...you have been grafted in among the others and now share in the nourishing sap from the olive root."** (Romans 11:17). The Greek word that describes the sap in this verse is *piotes* which means "plumpness; richness (oiliness); fatness."[43] The NIV translates this word as "nourishing" which refers to the sap the olive roots shares with the grafted-in branches. Nourishing roots contribute to health or growth. The Jewish people are the root of nourishment to the Gentiles as a mother's breast is to the suckling. The church needs this sap to remain healthy and grow. Without it, the church will be malnourished, weak, and lifeless.

Rejoice with Jerusalem and be glad for her, all you who love her; rejoice greatly with her, all you who mourn over her. For you will nurse and be satisfied at her comforting breasts; you will drink deeply and delight in her overwhelming abundance. (Isaiah 66:10-11 NIV)

What a great blessing the church has forfeited over the centuries! But this abundance will not come without first honoring God's chosen vessels.

The way a child treats his parents is an essential matter

---

[43] Strong, p.77

with God. From this relationship, the child receives his perception of authority for the rest of his life. This perception of authority will also affect the child's view of God's authority.

The church can be said to be a child of Mother Israel. The relationship that has been between the two since the New Covenant has not been healthy. More often than not, the church has dishonored her parent in rebellion and even persecution. And the result of this has been a distorted view of God's authority in the church.

These seeds of dishonor have infected the church with disrespect for God's law. This tendency of rebellion against God's authority or "Antinomianism" is rooted in the church's dishonor of her spiritual parent, Israel. Jude wrote to the church concerning those **"...who change the grace of our God into a license for immortality"** (Jude 4). The fruits of the church's anti-Semitism are evident.

The fifth commandment says, **"honor your father and mother, as the LORD your God commanded you, so that you may live long and that it may go well with you..."** (Exodus 5:16). Paul says that this **"...is the first commandment with a promise..."** (Ephesians 6:2). Let the church pursue this commandment and fully enter into this promise!

Chapter Eighty-Four

ISRAEL'S DESTINY

Without knowing the gift and call of the nation of Israel and their divine destiny amongst the nations, the church must stand corrected and repent. The promises for Israel have not been revoked but are on hold until they are taken by faith. The church must help the nation grow in faith so that the covenants of old may be fulfilled.

With the Messianic Jewish movement on the rise, the Gentile church soon will understand that **"...salvation has come to the Gentiles to make Israel envious"** (Romans 11:11 NIV). The Gentile church will not just acknowledge the Jew but will discover a deep appreciation and awe toward them. The church must remember that, speaking of the Jew:

Theirs is the adoption as sons; theirs the divine glory, the covenants, the receiving of the law, the temple worship, and the promises. Theirs are the patriarchs and from them is traced the human ancestry of Christ...." (Romans 9:4-5 NIV). Our God has purposed for the Jew to be the church's foundation. They were the womb in which Christianity was conceived.

The book of Isaiah reveals the heart of our God toward the nation of Israel:

Can a mother forget the baby at her breast and have no compassion for the child she has borne? Though she may

forget, I will not forget you! See, I have engraved you on the palms of my hand. (Isaiah 49:15-16 NIV)

The Lord has never forgotten his people, even throughout their darkest times. He is yearning for them to return to Him again. Hear the words of Jesus weeping over Israel:

O Jerusalem, Jerusalem, you who kill the prophets and stone those sent to you, how often I have longed to gather your children together, as a hen gathers her chicks under her wings, but you were not willing. (Matthew 23:37 NIV)

The Lord has preserved these people for a purpose: to bring salvation to the ends of the earth. And the church must do its part so that this can be fulfilled.

How good and pleasant it is when brothers live together in unity! It is like precious oil poured on the head, running down the beard, running down on Aaron's bread, down upon the collar of his robes. It is as if the dew of Hermon were failing on Mount Zion. For there the Lord bestows his blessing, even life forevermore. (Psalm 133 NIV).

A healthy relationship must exist between Israel and the church– one of understanding and appreciation for the gifts given to each by our God. The outcome of their oneness will be glorious!

When we fail to understand the role of Yahweh and Jesus from the Jewish perspective, we will not comprehend the God-ordained relationship between Jew and Gentile.

Chapter Eighty-Five

CYCLE KINGDOM

Once upon a time, in a distant kingdom, a king decreed that all those under his domain must ride unicycles. Those who used any bike with more than one wheel were excommunicated. The kingdom soon became converted to all unicyclists, and all others were driven out of this kingdom. The unicycle itself was the required mode of transportation, and every other kind of cycle was banished. The people proudly proclaimed, "Hear O nations, the true cycle is a unicycle, and all cycles must have one wheel only!'

For many centuries the kingdom existed as a kingdom of unicycles. Occasionally, there was chatter of a coming change to the domain. Curiously, many writings would be circulated amongst the unicyclists that another wheel would soon be added. The reports were trusted but often cloaked in mystery. Many interpreted these writings in anticipation of a shift in the kingdom of unicyclists, but few understood how and when it would happen.

Other nations soon challenged the isolated unicyclist kingdom. War soon broke out, and the unicycle kingdom became infiltrated by an evil empire that allowed all cyclists to ride freely in the land. The unicyclists attempted to fight off this oppressive kingdom, but all hopes of keeping the domain to

228

unicyclists only were lost. All cyclists rode freely, and the unicyclists began to hope for the coming change foretold in the ancient writings. They hoped the change would come and restore their kingdom to unicycles.

One day a man came to the kingdom riding a unicycle. He seemed different than everyone else in the domain and spoke with great authority. He told them that a new kingdom was coming, and he would soon point to the one who would usher in this new kingdom. The crowds excitedly waited for this person to be revealed, but the king of the old empire sought to have him put to death— but not before he pointed to the one the ancient writings had spoken.

The writings described a time when another wheel would be added to the cycle, and every cyclist must soon ride a bicycle. The one to bring to be the true king over the kingdom had to be born, and the people looked to him as the one to bring about something new. The unicyclists rejected his message and plotted to put him to death. But when they did, he came back to life and explained that all must ride a bicycle.

Many of his followers were strict unicyclists before his message. They immediately discovered the power and stability of a bicycle. Even those who previously believed in the possibility of many wheels on one cycle became convinced that the bicycle was the ordained cycle. The message spread rapidly in the unicyclist kingdom and throughout the world. Many unicyclists became convinced of the announcement of the bicycle— but most of the unicycle kingdom rejected what the ancient writings had said would come. Soon the unicyclist kingdom disintegrated even as the bicycle message spread rapidly.

About 350 years later, a new message started to rise in the nations that added another wheel to the bike. The tricycle was created, and pressure was put on many bicyclists to add another wheel to their bikes. The tri-cyclists noted that many people lost their balance on their bicycles, and a change was needed.

Even those of the unicyclist theory were told that the tricycle was really a unicycle with three wheels: One bike, but three wheels. They felt a connection to the unicycle kingdom and began to argue with the bicyclists fervently in favor of the tricycle. Nations even set up debates between bicyclists and tri-cyclists to settle the controversy. Years passed, and as the arguments continued, there would be no winner until one powerful nation decided to enforce tricycles as the way of all men. Those who would not comply would be excommunicated or killed. For over fifteen hundred years, all cycles were required to be tricycles, or the result would be imprisonment or even death.

Since then, few have been allowed to question the tricycle as the mode of transportation. The benefits of a stable third wheel make it safer than the bicycle– though the bike can reach much higher speeds. The bicycle requires one to balance their weight on the cycle, but the benefits far outweigh the tricycle and the unicycle. Soon a new season began for a fresh voice to arise and point people back to the original message. This new message will let go of some of the stability of the third wheel, and many will resist. The Creator did not frown upon the tricycle, but He is longing for the inhabitants of the world to learn how to ride a bicycle again.

Which theological cycle do you ride: a unicycle, a bicycle, or a tricycle? In other terms, I could ask, "Are you a Unitarian, Binitarian, or Trinitarian?" None of the preceding words are found in the Bible or on the lips of Jesus or the first disciples. They thought differently than we did and did not wonder about such questions.

Though the concepts might be brought out in the Bible, they should not be categorized or emphasized. The Bible is a book that uses relational language that describes a Father passing his kingdom on to His (One and Only) Unique Son. The introduction of philosophical language to Biblical terms is why the ideas of Unitarians, Binitarians, or Trinitarians are debated in modern theology.

I USED TO TEACH THAT GOD IS LIKE WATER: ONE SUBSTANCE BUT IN THREE SEPARATE STATES. WATER CAN BE A STEAM, A LIQUID, OR A SOLID CHUNK OF ICE, EACH STATE DEPENDENT UPON THE TEMPERATURE. BUT THIS EXAMPLE FROM NATURE FAILS TO EXPRESS THE MEANINGFUL RELATIONSHIP BETWEEN A FATHER AND A SON.

Chapter Eighty-Six

ONE THRONE

To sum up, this book would be to say that the Jews in the times of Jesus tended to believe in the idea of the two powers of heaven over the strict monotheism that is in Judaism today. Jesus is the second power of heaven, and though monotheism lacks emphasis, "mono-throne-ism" does not. Monothronism is the idea that there is only one throne on which the two powers of heaven sit.

I have many friends who are Oneness Pentecostals and many friends who are Trinitarians. I feel Jesus in them and their meetings, even though neither group holds to my understanding of the two powers of heaven. My question is: "How can Jesus show up in their midst even though they do not see eye to eye on the definition of monotheism?" If getting monotheism right is not the reason why Jesus is showing up in their midst, then what is?

Jesus is honored in the same way that the Father is honored by Oneness Pentecostals and Trinitarians. If this principle is violated, the presence of Jesus will be removed.

ALL MAY HONOR THE SON JUST AS THEY HONOR THE FATHER.

Chapter Eighty-Seven

HIGH CHRISTOLOGY

My journey has been to discover which belief in history has the most biblically accurate Christology. I have a member at my church who was raised in both Oneness Pentecostal churches and Trinitarian churches. Her heart was to please the Lord in what she believed. Her genuine search for truth was a struggle because she only had two options. Neither stance entirely made sense to her, but her heart was to understand. After reading my first book, Heaven's Dynasty, she realized there was another alternative belief that could be seen as the Biblical narrative of Scripture.

When we study the Scriptures, we should ask ourselves, "What determines orthodoxy?"

    1. Christology (The Study of the Christ)

    2. Pneumatology (The Study of the Spirit)

    3. Theology (The Study of the Father)

Christology must be our primary emphasis above all other studies. How we perceive Jesus determines how the kingdom will advance. A Jehovah Witness will not worship Jesus and will only worship Yahweh/Jehovah.

Since the 4th Century, there has been a deep commitment by most of the Western church to identify only Trinitarians as fully orthodox. In 381 C.E., the Roman Emperor Theodosius

233

declared that true Christians were only those who believed in the single divinity of the Father, Son, and Holy Spirit with an equal majesty. Similarly, many Oneness Pentecostals have suggested that only those who speak in tongues are saved and have the Spirit. It is time we are sure to hold to a proper Christology and allow that to determine one's orthodoxy.

THE MOVEMENT OF THE SPIRIT THAT BEGAN IN THE EARLY 20TH CENTURY AT ASUZA STREET, DIVIDED WITHIN THE FIRST DECADE OVER A REVELATION THAT CAME ABOUT CONCERNING 'THE NAME OF THE FATHER AND THE SON AND THE HOLY SPIRIT'. THE REVELATION THAT SPLIT THE MOVEMENT WAS THAT THE NAME SPOKEN OF IN MATTHEW 28:20 WAS THE NAME OF JESUS. IN THE PENTECOSTAL MOVEMENT TODAY, WE HAVE "ONENESS" PENTECOSTALS OR "JESUS ONLY" CHRISTIANS, WHO CLAIM THAT JESUS IS THE FATHER, THE SON, AND THE SPIRIT.

Chapter Eighty-Eight

RENEWED COVENANT

Christianity is a river that streams out of the rich heritage of the Old Testament. Too many teachers in the body of Christ disconnect the first 39 books of the Bible from the last 27 books. If your version of Christianity is not rooted in the writings of the ancient Jew, your faith will be found lacking. The New Covenant is a renewed covenant that was prophesied about in Jeremiah 31:31,33:

Behold, the days are coming, declares the LORD, when I will make a new covenant with the house of Israel and the house of Judah... I will put my law within them, and I will write it on their hearts. And I will be their God, and they shall be my people. (Jeremiah 31:31,33)

The Hebrew word *hadas* refers to making something new, renewing or restoring it. Josiah restores or renews the temple is another time the word *hadas* is used (2 Chronicles 24:4). The New Covenant or Testament might better be called the Renewed or Restored Covenant or Testament. We should read the Renewed Testament through the eyes of the Old Testament for deeper understanding.

As the disciples walked unknowingly with Jesus on the road to Emmaus, He said to them:

"How foolish you are, and how slow to believe all that the

prophets have spoken! Did not the Messiah have to suffer these things and then enter his glory?" And beginning with Moses and all the Prophets, he explained to them what was said in all the Scriptures concerning himself.

(Luke 24:25-27 NIV)

Would Modern Bible teachers be uncomfortable with Jesus using the Old Testament to explain Himself? Are our churches full of people who Jesus would say are foolish and slow to believe? Christians can become wise and full of faith if they ground themselves in the Old and New Testaments.

Jesus in the New Testament is the same Jesus of the Old Testament. Jesus is not Yahweh but the son of Yahweh. The first disciples of Jesus did not struggle with worshipping and honoring the son of Yahweh. They declared Jesus as Lord and understood he was sitting on the throne of his Father.

Most Christians today struggle with accepting the idea of two powers in heaven because of the fear of violating monotheism. Yet, as some of the top Jewish scholars now recognize the two powers in heaven concept was a commonly accepted idea of Jewish people in the time of Jesus.

RABBIS THROUGHOUT THE CENTURIES HAVE EMPHASIZED THE ONENESS OF GOD. THE REAL BIBLICAL EMPHASIS IS NOT HIS SINGULARITY, BUT RATHER HIS DESIRE TO BE ONE IN COVENANT.

Chapter Eighty-Nine

THE ASCENSION

One topic in theology that was not touched upon often in my theological training was the ascension of Jesus. We understand that Jesus ascended to the throne of the kingdom at Pentecost. As Solomon ascended to the throne of his father David, Jesus ascended to His Father's throne.

The ascension seems a lousy strategy. It's as if our best player was substituted just as the game began. The early church lost its leader, but His mantle would be multiplied upon his followers. After Jesus' resurrection and prior to His ascension, He was with his disciples for forty days.

During forty days, He presented Himself alive to them after his suffering by many proofs, appearing to them and speaking about the kingdom of God. (Acts 1:3 NIV) Jesus was preparing them for His ascension to heaven and for the kingdom of God to come to earth in power. **"Then he appeared to more than five hundred brothers at one time..."** (1 Corinthians 15:6). Imagine Jesus revealing Himself visibly to five hundred people at one time. Do it again, Lord!

Jesus was taken up on day forty, and the Holy Spirit came upon the disciples on day fifty.

And when he had said these things, as they were looking on, he was lifted up, and a cloud took him out of their sight.

(Acts 1:9 NIV)

Where did Jesus go? Jesus ascended to assume his seat at the right hand of the Father.

So, then the Lord Jesus, after he had spoken to them, was taken up into heaven and sat down at the right hand of God.

(Mark 16:19 NIV)

The ascension is the enthronement of Jesus, which ignites the church's mission. Heaven's strategy was that once Jesus was seated on the throne, his Spirit and anointing could be placed upon his followers. The kingdom could now advance on earth unhindered through the name of King Jesus.

THE ANOINTING INCLUDES THE RECOGNITION THAT WE ARE PART OF THE DYNASTY PASSED ON TO US FROM THE FATHER HIMSELF. HE IS NOT WITHHOLDING HIS KINGDOM FROM HIS CHILDREN. HE FREELY AND HAPPILY GIVES IT! "DO NOT BE AFRAID, LITTLE FLOCK, FOR YOUR FATHER HAS BEEN PLEASED TO GIVE YOU THE KINGDOM" (LUKE 12:32–33) THE GENERATIONAL BLESSING THAT IS IMPARTED FROM FATHER TO SON IS THE MODEL IN WHICH THE KINGDOM IS NOW ADVANCING ON EARTH. IN EVERY DECISION WE MAKE, WE MUST ASK GOD FOR THE AWARENESS OF HOW WE ARE AFFECTING THE COMING GENERATIONS.

Chapter Ninety

THE B TEAM

The ascension is the story of the body of Jesus moving to heaven. It is not escaping from the bodily realm but the entry of humanity– in our physicalness – into heaven, the sphere of God. Flesh and bone will take the throne.

Just as we have borne the image of the man of dust, we shall also bear the image of the man of heaven. (1 Corinthians 15:49 ESV)

The ascension of Jesus is the foretaste of the ascension of a new humanity to our royal status. Human flesh is now with our God Himself. The 1st Reformation sparked in 1517 AD with Martin Luther, who proclaimed justification by faith against the works-based salvation of the Catholic church. The 2nd Reformation is happening five hundred years later, announcing not only justification by faith but also glorification by faith.

But you will receive power when the Holy Spirit has come upon you, and you will be my witnesses in Jerusalem and in all Judea and Samaria, and to the end of the earth (Acts 1:8 NIV).

In America, sports teams have 'A' and 'B' teams. The 'B' team played once the 'A' team had sealed the victory. Jesus sealed our victory, and we are the 'B' team finishing the game on the field. We have Jesus' anointing and His Spirit to carry us through.

He who believes in me, as the Scripture has said, from within him will flow rivers of living water." But he said this about the Spirit, which those believing in him were to receive. For the Holy Spirit was not yet given, because Jesus(Yahweh will save) was not yet glorified. (John 7:38-39 TNT)

The embodied Christ absent in that body is present with us through the Spirit. As the ascended king, Jesus sends us to proclaim His reign to the world through the power of the Spirit.

For those whom he foreknew he also predestined to be conformed to the image of his Son, in order that he might be the firstborn among many brothers. And those whom he predestined he also called, and those whom he called he also justified, and those whom he justified he also glorified. (Romans 8:29-30 ESV)

You and I are conformed to the image of His Son, and now that we are justified, we must also recognize we have been glorified. All theology is in the tense of the verbs. The '-ed' ending signifies it has already happened in the past, and now we must receive it by faith.

"EVERYONE WHO FALLS ON THAT STONE WILL BE BROKEN TO PIECES, BUT HE ON WHOM IT FALLS WILL BE CRUSHED" (LUKE 20:18) . FALLING ON JESUS IS THAT PLACE OF TOTAL SURRENDER. NO MORE STRIVING. "IT IS FINISHED!"

Chapter Ninety-One

GOD ENCOUNTERS

Jacob had many powerful God encounters during his life. He experienced several dreams and other mystical experiences where he saw both Yahweh and the Angel-Yahweh. Jacob's first encounter happened after leaving his family on his journey to find a bride. The Bible tells us that Jacob fell asleep, and he dreamed.

And behold, a stairway set upon the earth, and its top reached to heaven. Behold, the angels of God ascending and descending on it. Behold, Yahweh(*Jealous one*) stood above it.
(Genesis 28:12-13 TNT)

The dream speaks of angels or messengers ascending and descending. Note the direction– first from earth to heaven, then from heaven back down to earth. Was this angelic activity being sent to heaven to retrieve what we need, or is this man's invitation to ascend into heaven for resources? Jesus uses this story and declares His own authority over heaven and earth.

Truly, truly, I say to you, you will see heaven opened, and the angels of God ascending and descending on the Son of Man.
(John 1:51 ESV)

Jacob's first encounter left him forever changed. As he wakes up, he declares that **"Surely Yahweh(*Jealous one*) is in this place, and I did not know it"** (vs. 16). Like Jacob, we often become

241

unaware of the presence of Yahweh in our midst because of our anxiety from the past and our fear of the future. Jacobs decides to make a covenant with the God of his fathers at this moment. I think the fear of the LORD came over him at this moment.

He was afraid, and said, "How dreadful is this place! This is none other than the house of our God, and this is the gate of heaven." (Genesis 28:17 TNT)

Jacob realizes he is where Yahweh is, and He has found the gateway of heaven. The presence of Yahweh can be discovered when this gate is opened. Jesus said, **"I am the gate; whoever enters through me will be saved"** (John 10:9 NIV).

First-century believers were known as those "...who belonged to the Way" (Acts 9:2) . But the Way had to remain closed until the flaming sword of judgment had fallen upon Jesus for mankind. Jesus was the Gate (John 10:7) and the Way (John 14:6) . The Way brought God and man back together in fellowship. The first gate placed at the entrance of Eden forever reminded man of the price of breaking covenant. It was a restraint upon mankind—a source of necessary frustration for a time—but, as a tollgate remains shut until the toll is paid, so the first gate remained shut until Jesus paid the toll.

Chapter Ninety-Two

AWAKENING

Jacob then quickly built an altar and changed the name of the place in which he had his encounter.

He called the name of that place Bethel(*House of God*), but the name of the city was Luz(*Almond tree*) at the first.

(Genesis 28:19 TNT)

Every house or dwelling place where our God dwells begins with an awakening. Interestingly, the almond tree was the first to awaken from winter's sleep and blossom. As Jacob was awakened to the presence of Yahweh, he then made a covenant vow. Every relationship is made secure through covenant.

Jacob(Heel grabber) vowed a vow, saying, "If this God will be with me, and will keep me in this way that I go, and will give me bread to eat, and clothing to put on, so that I come again to my father's house in peace, and Yahweh(*Jealous one*) will be my God, then this stone, which I have set up for a pillar, will be the house of my God. Of all that you will give me I will surely give a tenth to you." (Genesis 28:20-22 TNT)

Here are the five things that Jacob believes in as he commits to giving a tenth of everything he has back to Yahweh.

1. **Presence–** "...be with me."
2. **Protection–** "...keep me in this way."
3. **Provision–** "...give me bread and clothing."

243

4. Providence– "…come again to my father s house."

5. Peace– "…return in peace."

Jacob later arrives at the house of Laban, his future father-in-law, who is ten times the trickster that Jacob ever was. Under Laban's leadership, he is treated unfairly, but instead of grabbing at the heel of man, he follows the direction of his God.

EVERY DECISION YOU MAKE IS LIKE CUTTING THE PIE. COVENANTS WERE MADE OR 'CUT' IN THE OLD TESTAMENT. THE KNIFE WAS THE TOOL THAT EMPOWERED THE COVENANT. BAD DECISIONS WILL KEEP YOU FROM FULFILLING YOUR COVENANT OBLIGATIONS. BECAUSE THERE IS ONLY SO MUCH OF MY PIE TO GO AROUND, IF I GIVE SOMEONE OR SOMETHING A BIGGER PORTION, SOMEONE ELSE WILL GET A SMALLER SLICE. EACH OF US MUST KNOW THE SIZE OF THEIR PIE! KNOWING THE SIZE OF YOUR PIE GIVES YOU AN OVERVIEW ON HOW EACH OF YOUR DECISIONS SHOULD BE MADE. IT HELPS YOU SAY "NO" WHEN YOU NEED TO. WHEN YOU FAIL TO MAKE THE PROPER CUT, YOU ARE NOT HONORING YOUR COVENANT OBLIGATIONS. PORTION SIZES RELATE TO COVENANT OBLIGATIONS. THE TITHE IS THE LORD'S PORTION OF YOUR FINANCES. IT IS NEVER OUR TITHE. IT IS HIS PORTION.

Chapter Ninety-Three

YOUR NAME PLEASE?

Jacob shares his story about how he received the revelation to prosper in a difficult time. His cruel father-in-law had changed his wages seven times, and without supernatural intervention, he would have never flourished! Below is the dream he received.

The angel of our God said to me in the dream, "Jacob(*Heel grabber*)," and I said, "Here I am." He said..., "I am the God of Bethel(House of God), where you anointed a pillar, where you vowed a vow to me. Now arise, get out from this land, and return to the land of your birth." (Genesis 31:10-13 TNT) The angel of God in this verse says, **"I am the God of Bethel!"** We would assume Yahweh would be the God of Bethel. But instead, this angel is who is present, protecting, providing, providentially guiding, and bringing peace to Jacob according to his vow. The pre-incarnate Jesus is the other power of heaven.

Jacob's subsequent encounter brought him a name change from Jacob to Israel. This name means "struggle with God." Yahweh gave the name to his people to remind them that He desires us to struggle with our God until we overcome. Yahweh invites us to wrestle with Him until our name is changed from Jacob, which means "Heel grabber." It reveals to us that we are schemers and tricksters hoping to get our way through our devilish schemes.

245

When Jacob was hours away from meeting his estranged brother, who had once wanted him dead, he emptied himself, sending everything he had across the river. At the ford of Jabbok, which means 'emptied,' he has an encounter.

He sent over all his possessions. So, Jacob was left alone, and a man wrestled with him till daybreak. When the man saw that he could not overpower him, he touched the socket of Jacob's hip so that his hip was wrenched as he wrestled with the man. Then the man said, "Let me go, for it is daybreak."(Genesis 32:23-26 NIV 84)

This wrestling match is where the Israelites received their name and their calling. Here it describes Jacob's encounter. But the struggle was not with Yahweh; it was with a man, who was also called both a God and an angel in the book of Hosea.

In the womb he took his brother by the heel; and in his manhood he contended with our God. Indeed, he struggled with the angel, and prevailed; he wept, and made supplication to him. (Hosea 12:3-4 TNT)

Who is this heavenly wrestler: a man, a God, and an angel? Why does this wrestling match result in a blessing, a name change, and a limp? The father of all the tribes of Israel had an encounter with Jesus, though Jacob could not get His name. His name was not yet to be revealed for another 2000 years. But Jacob did not let go until he received his blessing.

But Jacob replied, "I will not let you go unless you bless me." The man asked him, "What is your name?" "Jacob," he answered. Then the man said, "Your name will no longer be

Jacob, but Israel, because you have struggled with God and with humans and have overcome." Jacob said, "Please tell me your name." But he replied, "Why do you ask my name?" Then he blessed him there. So, Jacob called the place Peniel, saying, "It is because I saw our God face to face, and yet my life was spared." (Genesis 32:26-30 NIV 84)

Jacob knew he was not wrestling with a mere man– he saw our God face to face. The identity of this mysterious figure that wrestles with Jacob is noted in Scripture:

1) **A man** (Genesis 32:28)

2) **A God** (Genesis 32:30; Hosea 12:3)

3) **An angel** (Hosea 12:4)

Yet the one with whom Jacob wrestled never revealed His name. We read that Jacob could no longer walk without limping after this encounter. **"The sun rose above him as he passed Peniel(Face of God), and he was limping because of his hip"** (Genesis 32:31 TNT). The Jewish people will continue to limp until they know the name of the One with whom they are wrestling! His name is Jesus.

Chapter Ninety-Four

A DIM MIRROR

Three theologians came together before their king to discuss an issue about which each had reached a different conclusion. The king told them a story as they argued and debated the topic. He said:

Three men were standing in a dark room together when a voice alerted them that a diamond would be dropped on the floor in their midst. Each man went to his knees, frantically searching for the diamond, and once they believed that they had it in their possession, boasted to the other of their find. Yet the room remained dark, and only at daylight would each honestly know which of them had found the diamond and which of them were grasping a useless pebble.

Paul wrote to the Corinthians in the love chapter:

Now we see in a mirror dimly, but then face to face. Now I know in part; then I shall know fully, even as I have been fully known. (1 Corinthians 13:12 ESV).

Like the story above, some of us shouting, "I have a diamond! I have a diamond!" may be surprised at daylight to find a useless pebble in our hands. Now the mirror is dim, and we see in part, but one day we will fully know.

Reading the Bible with a different narrative is like taking a journey across the United States. There are many other roads one could travel to arrive at a destination. There will be some incredible scenery and some traffic jams as well. And on every trip, there are some significant bumps in the road. None of these can be avoided– whether journeying across the United States or developing your own theology. The goal is to find the path with the best scenery and the least number of potholes.

EVEN A BROKEN CLOCK IS RIGHT TWICE A DAY.

Chapter Ninety-Five

CONCLUSION

Rabbi Daniel Boyarin defines three notions that he found common with Christianity and 2nd Temple Judaism(Judaism from the times of Ezra to the destruction of the Temple in 70 A.D.)

1) A dual godhead with a Father and a Son

2) A Redeemer who himself will be both God and man

3) A Redeemer would suffer and die as part of the salvational process.

Boyarin's discoveries affirm what I believe to be the most accurate description of Jewish thought in the times of Jesus. What was later deemed by Jewish leaders of the 1st Century as the two-power heresy was the respected Biblical paradigm of its day.

I stand on the shoulders of others who have gone before me and have done the work of digging up and discovering the riches of revelation. Great men like Daniel Wallace, Daniel Boyarin, and Alan Segal provided the necessary historical and scholarly foundation on which these ideas can firmly stand.

No building can stand without a firm foundation. I conclude that the belief that two powers existed in heaven was the predominant belief in the time of Jesus. This understanding provided the foundation for the Biblical authors' revelation. John wrote in his gospel: **"And this is eternal life, that they know you, the only true God, and Jesus Christ whom you have sent"** (John 17:3 ESV). Simply put, eternal life is knowing these two powers in heaven.

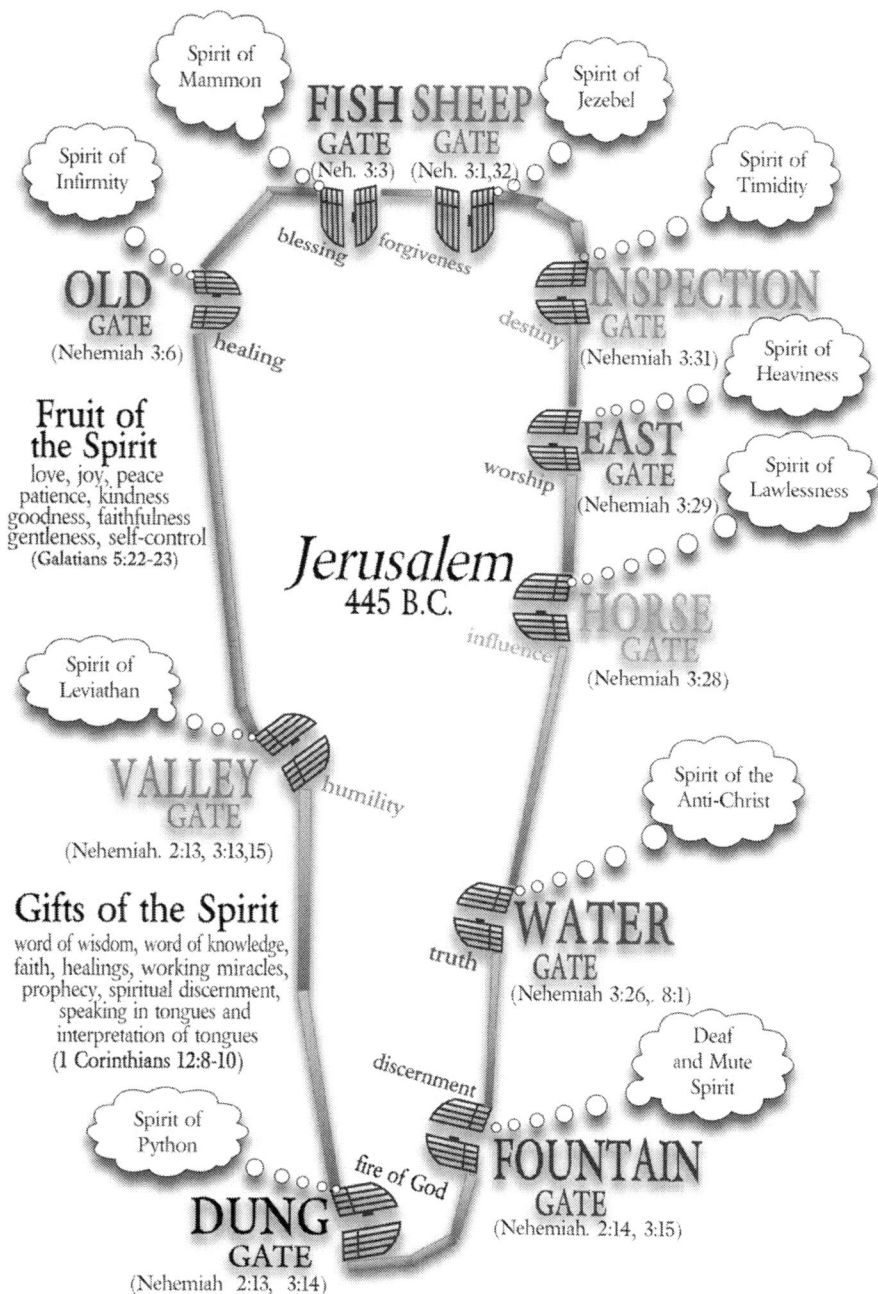

Spirit of Mammon

FISH GATE (Neh. 3:3)

SHEEP GATE (Neh. 3:1,32)

Spirit of Jezebel

Spirit of Infirmity

Spirit of Timidity

blessing

forgiveness

OLD GATE (Nehemiah 3:6)

healing

destiny

INSPECTION GATE (Nehemiah 3:31)

Spirit of Heaviness

Fruit of the Spirit
love, joy, peace
patience, kindness
goodness, faithfulness
gentleness, self-control
(Galatians 5:22-23)

worship

EAST GATE (Nehemiah 3:29)

Spirit of Lawlessness

Jerusalem
445 B.C.

influence

HORSE GATE (Nehemiah 3:28)

Spirit of Leviathan

VALLEY GATE (Nehemiah. 2:13, 3:13,15)

humility

Spirit of the Anti-Christ

Gifts of the Spirit
word of wisdom, word of knowledge,
faith, healings, working miracles,
prophecy, spiritual discernment,
speaking in tongues and
interpretation of tongues
(1 Corinthians 12:8-10)

truth

WATER GATE (Nehemiah 3:26,. 8:1)

Deaf and Mute Spirit

discernment

Spirit of Python

fire of God

DUNG GATE (Nehemiah 2:13, 3:14)

FOUNTAIN GATE (Nehemiah. 2:14, 3:15)

MAP OF JERUSALEM

1. The Sheep Gate: Forgiveness
Father, I thank you for showing your mercy to _____ and covering them in the blood of Jesus. I pronounce their sins forgiven and declare freedom from every anxious thought and accusation of the enemy. INVITE: FRUIT OF THE SPIRIT FORBID: SPIRIT OF JEZEBEL
(love, joy, peace, patience, kindness, goodness, faithfulness, gentleness, self-control)

2. The Fish Gate: Blessing
I pray for provision and blessing over _____. I thank you for supplying all that they need for the vision on their life today. Free them from poverty thinking and surround them with generosity. INVITE: PROSPERITY FORBID: SPIRIT OF MAMMON

3. The Old Gate: Healing
Father, I thank you for healing _____ today. Refresh them and allow them to experience and release healing– physically, emotionally, and spiritually-everywhere they go.
INVITE: HEALING FORBID: SPIRIT OF INFIRMITY

4. The Valley Gate: Humility
I thank You for _____ walking in humility and living in total dependence on You. Allow them to receive everything they need for life and godliness as they fully possess the nature of Christ. INVITE: YAHWEH TO SLAY THE SPIRIT OF LEVIATHAN

5. The Dung Gate: Fire of God
Father, I thank you for your protection over _____. Cleanse them from all bitterness and every fleshly desire and ungodly attitude. I declare they are illegal territory for Satan and the kingdom of darkness. INVITE: THRONE ROOM CONFIDENCE FORBID: SPIRIT OF PYTHON

6. The Fountain Gate: Spiritual Sight
Father, I pray you give _____ clear direction and vision for this day. I pray for angelic activity over their life as You guide them. May the inward flow of Your Spirit outweigh any trial or struggle they are facing in their life and give them increasing discernment today.
INVITE: GIFTS OF THE SPIRIT FORBID: DEAF AND MUTE SPIRIT
(word of wisdom, word of knowledge, faith, healings, prophecy, working of miracles, spiritual discernment, interpretation of tongues, speaking in tongues)

7. The Water Gate: The Word and Spirit
Father, I declare that _____ will know Your voice and will possess an increasing hunger for Your Word. May they receive fresh revelation and powerful insight today.
INVITE: SPIRIT OF TRUTH FORBID: SPIRIT OF THE ANTICHRIST

8. The Horse Gate: Influence
Father, I thank you for the fear of the LORD over _____ and for keeping them strong in the midst of ungodly influences. Set them ablaze with love, overflowing in power and self-control. INVITE: OPEN DOORS/ BOLDNESS FORBID: SPIRIT OF LAWLESSNESS

9. The East Gate: Worship
Father, I thank you for allowing Jesus to be central to _____. Give them a joyous, thankful heart today. Let the weight of Your glory cover them today.
INVITE: FREEDOM FORBID: SPIRIT OF HEAVINESS

1o. The Inspection Gate: Destiny
Father, I thank you for the destiny of _____ being fulfilled. I pray for godly connections in their life as they grow in the wisdom of You. I thank you for the books of heaven being revealed to them and their skills being developed to prepare them to walk out their destiny.
INVITE: DIVINE APPOINTMENTS FORBID: SPIRIT OF TIMIDITY

DECLARATIONS BASED ON THE GATES

1. The Sheep Gate: Forgiveness
I am the righteousness of God in Christ Jesus. As I have been fully forgiven,
I chose to forgive and to show mercy to others. I cast down every accusation, lie and
anxious thought over my life. INVITE: FRUIT OF THE SPIRIT FORBID: SPIRIT OF JEZEBEL
(love, joy, peace, patience, kindness, goodness, faithfulness, gentleness, self-control)

2. The Fish Gate: Blessing
In every area of my life, I live in abundance. I am seated at my Father's table with everything
I need for this day. I am highly valued in heaven, and I overflow in wisdom and generosity
when making financial and spiritual decisions. I am free from all worry and poverty thinking.
INVITE: PROSPERITY FORBID: SPIRIT OF MAMMON

3. The Old Gate: Healing
I walk in ever-increasing health– energized to accomplish everything I need to do this day.
Every person I lay my hands upon will be healed and freed from the power of the devil.
 INVITE: HEALING FORBID: SPIRIT OF INFIRMITY

4. The Valley Gate: Humility
I celebrate the opportunity today to live a life of total dependence on You. As I humble
myself, You are lifting me up to new levels of grace and opportunity. I break off the power of
pride, control, and selfishness over my life. INVITE: YAHWEH TO SLAY THE SPIRIT OF LEVIATHAN

5. The Dung Gate: Fire of God
My soul belongs to the living God, and I am illegal territory for Satan and his kingdom. I am
a partaker in the divine nature of Christ and have the authority to cast out demons and to
raise the dead. INVITE: THRONE ROOM CONFIDENCE FORBID: SPIRIT OF PYTHON

6. The Fountain Gate: Spiritual Sight
I am full of God's Spirit, and I have been given divine strategies and heavenly creativity for
my life and for the lives of others. I was created to see clearly into the spiritual realm and to
walk in discernment. INVITE: GIFTS OF THE SPIRIT FORBID: DEAF AND MUTE SPIRIT
(word of wisdom, word of knowledge, faith, healings, prophecy, working of miracles,
spiritual discernment, interpretation of tongues, speaking in tongues)

7. The Water Gate: The Word and the Spirit
It is easy for me to hear the voice of God. Every time I open the Bible, I receive fresh
revelation and powerful insight. I was created to experience dreams, visions, and angelic
encounters. INVITE: SPIRIT OF TRUTH FORBID: SPIRIT OF THE ANTICHRIST

8. The Horse Gate: Influence
I am highly motivated to share the gospel. The world will not influence me, but I will
influence the world. I will be led out of temptation and will be delivered from all evil.
Because of Jesus, my influence will be felt for hundreds of years.
INVITE: OPEN DOORS/ BOLDNESS FORBID: SPIRIT OF LAWLESSNESS

9. The East Gate: Worship
Right now, I demolish any lack of enthusiasm I have about worshipping Jesus. I am a temple
of skin, a place where God dwells and where Jesus is continually worshipped.
INVITE: FREEDOM/JOY FORBID: THE SPIRIT OF HEAVINESS

10. The Inspection Gate: Destiny
The decisions I make today are producing blessing for my future generations. I was created
to fulfill my destiny and to be joined together with others who will do the same. May my
God-given skills increase and further develop as I carry contagious hope and increasing favor.
INVITE: DIVINE APPOINTMENTS FORBID: SPIRIT OF TIMIDITY

Chris Monaghan and his wife, Debbie, live near Richmond, Indiana, U.S.A. Chris is the Senior Leaders of Gateway Church and lead translator of the Name Translation Bible (TNT). Chris is also the co-founder of the Gateway Hunger Relief Center that feeds over 700 families each month in his region. With American Democracy being challenged in these times, Chris is a founding leader of the Voice of the Patriots– a grassroots, regional organization working to inform Americans about the truth of what is really behind mask and COVID vaccinations as being government mandates that infringe on constitutional freedoms. Chris and Debbie believe in equipping every believer to do what Jesus did and his focus is on changing atmospheres of cities through worship, teaching and humanitarian acts. Chris has traveled to three continents, and regularly sees physical and emotional healings take place, Chris has authored six books and has written more than 25 worship songs. Chris is a graduate of Penn State University, has a Master of Biblical Studies from Messiah Biblical Institute, and has taught and studied at many other Seminaries and Bible schools. Chris and his wife, Debbie also serve as coordinators for Family Foundations International and help facilitate emotional healing through their seminars. Chris and Debbie have five children and two grandchildren.

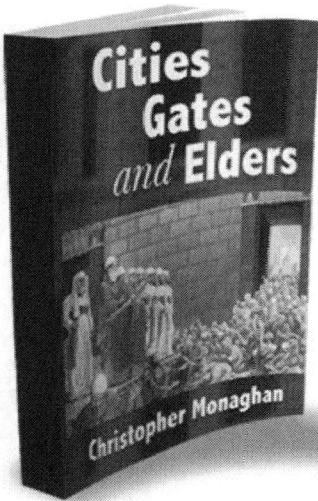

Cities, Gates, and Elders answers the question of why Jesus told Peter, **"...upon this rock I will build my church; and the gates of hell shall not prevail against it"** (Matthew 16:18). The disciples of Jesus understood that the gates were gateways in which the elders of the city would sit and judge. The decisions made at these gates had authoritative power over regions. Jesus was saying that the decisions made in hell would not prevail against the decisions made on earth by His people. *Available in paperback or digital format through Amazon.*

If you were to open up a Hebrew dictionary, you would discover the first word is father. The Hebrew language begins with the most important word you will ever need to know. Heaven's Dynasty rediscovers the Father emphasis each of us need to have in our daily lives and the understanding of how to pass on the generational blessing as God did Himself to His Son. Do you know God as Father? Do you understand how powerful it is to have God as your Father? *Available in paperback or digital format through Amazon.*

Gatekeepers and Watchman on the Wall is a journey around the walls of Jerusalem and a discovery of how each gate applies to our spiritual journey. The ten gates reveal hidden truths found in the book of Nehemiah chapter 3 for us to discover. In fifty-two days, Nehemiah rebuilt the walls and set the gates back up in Jerusalem. And just as Nehemiah, with efficient intent, finished his work quickly, you can do the same as you discover each gate has a spiritual significance. *Available in paperback or digital format through Amazon.*

Often prayer is more obligation and guilt driven than joy and result driven. This book is my journey to pray with confidence and boldness. I have taught classes on prayer and preached countless messages on prayer, but I also pray daily and consistently because of the principles found in this writing. Prayer is a beautiful gift and compelling invitation that every child of God has been offered. You and I have been invited into this position of privilege and honor. *Available in paperback or digital format through Amazon.*

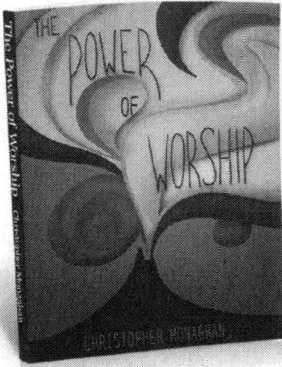

Few realize the power available to all who will worship as act of devotion- not just emotion. Throughout the Bible there are countless stories of miraculous breakthroughs that take place because of the realization that worship will shift the atmosphere wherever you are! The truths found in this book will help you bring heaven to earth on a daily basis. Chris has lead worship teams for over twenty-five years and has written and recorded dozens of worship songs. This book will help you understand the spiritual significance of worship. *Available in paperback or digital format through Amazon.*

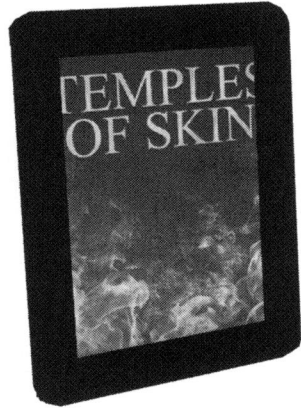

Temples of skin is a course based on our call to become a skin temple in which the LORD can dwell. Each chapter addresses key components that will allow the worshipper to grow and mature. Worship is one activity that we do here on earth that will continue throughout eternity. Until the church embraces the power of worship, she will never reach her full potential. This manual is written to give you a Biblical foundation of what worship should look like. This handbook includes 10 lessons and study questions that you and other worshippers can use in a Bible study or small group. *Available in paperback or digital format through Amazon.*

Christopher Monaghan

The LORD Himself declared His intension to dwell in something He made and not something man made. The word is *acheiropoietos* which is derived from two words: The idea that God desired to live in temples of skin(what He made) and not in temples of stone(made by human hands) is a central thought in much of the Bible. Skin Temples is an invitation for God Himself to come inhabit in what He has made with His hands: us! Skin Temples is a full-length worship project that Chris recorded to capture his heart for Jesus through music. *Available on Spotify, Amazon, iTunes, and YouTube.*

Simply I Come is a collection of six powerful acoustic songs of worship and praise. We feel that there are two things that distinguish Simply I Come from most projects. The first is that the sessions were a time of fellowship and worship first and foremost. Our primary desire and focus in the studio was to lift our hearts and voices to God. The second thing is the unique voice and gifting of the participants. Simply I Come is the collaborative effort of leaders and worshipers, who brought the best of their God given talent to the project. *Available on Spotify, Amazon, iTunes, and YouTube.*

OTHER RESOURCES

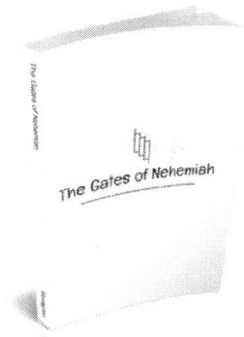

Got prayer? Prayer is a beautiful gift and compelling invitation that every child of God has been offered. If you want to change the future, you must disturb the present. Prayer creates a disturbance in the kingdom of darkness because it stirs up heaven to move. You and I have been invited into this position of privilege and honor. History belongs to us because we will pray and not give up. Take this 13-week video course along with the workbook. *Available in paperback or digital format through Amazon.*

The Gates of Nehemiah Study Guide is a journey around the gates of Jerusalem during the time of Nehemiah. Based on Nehemiah the third chapter, this study guide allows you to develop ten daily declarations and ten prayer focuses based upon each of the ten gates. This is one of the most detailed studies available on the Gates of Jerusalem in the times of Nehemiah. Available as an 11-week video study that gives an overview and a teaching on each gate. Discover a new paradigm of prayer and declarations that will enrich your quiet time with the Lord on a daily basis.

OTHER RESOURCES

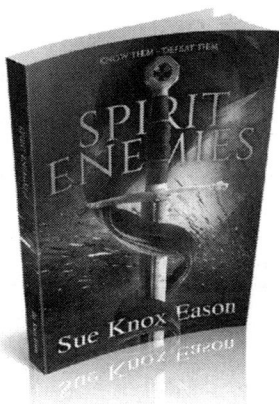

Online Courses by Chris Monaghan
Sign up at www.igateway.org

As we have worked on the Name Translation Bible, we discovered that every name in the Bible is significant. The Israelites had to overcome many different people groups to possess their land, each group is symbolic of something each of us will face on our journey into the Promised Land. Sue's book is titled, "Spirit Enemies: Know Them–Defeat Them." Pick up your staff and sword, and begin this journey to possess your Promised Land! *Available in paperback or digital format through Amazon.*

Jesus has not hidden his truths from us. He has hidden them for us. You will discover how to live a supernatural, authentic, transforming and connected life through theses teachings. The Bible is not a rule book–it is a book that teaches you how to rule. Gateway Equip is an online school that will allow you to take these powerful teachings with you wherever you are. The school has a downloadable app to listen on the go or you can log in on your computer.

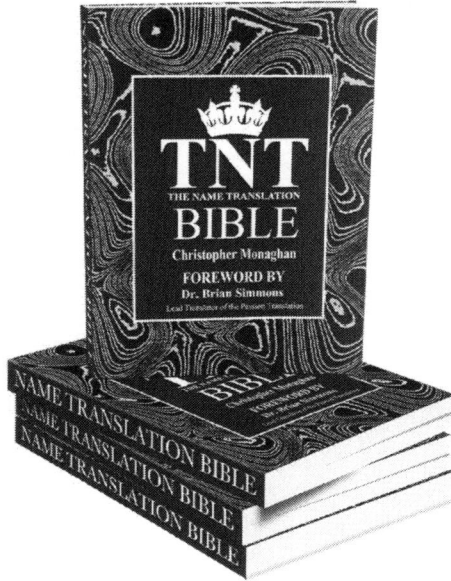

The Name Translation (TNT) of the Bible presents the meaning of every proper name in the Scriptures. In ancient thought, names are more than identifiers, but instead point to the destiny of that which was named. The Bible often tells us the meaning of a name of a person or place to help us remember the story we are reading. Until now, the meanings of the names needed to be researched in each verse of the Bible to grow our understanding of the word of God. The Name Translation inserts the meaning of every proper name in parentheses next to each proper name in every verse of the Bible. Names are keys that help us unlock destinies. The Name Translation allows the reader to connect each name in context to the Biblical narrative as it was original written without having to learn Greek or Hebrew. The TNT is a powerful tool for personal study and for teaching the truths found in the Bible. *Available in paperback or digital format through Amazon.*

Printed in Great Britain
by Amazon

16269394R00151